Werner by Lord Byron

or, The Inheritance

A TRAGEDY

George Gordon Byron, 6th Baron Byron, but more commonly known as just Byron was a leading English poet in the Romantic Movement along with Keats and Shelley.

Byron was born on January 22nd, 1788. He was a great traveller across Europe, spending many years in Italy and much time in Greece. With his aristocratic indulgences, flamboyant style along with his debts, and a string of lovers he was the constant talk of society.

In 1823 he joined the Greeks in their war of Independence against the Ottoman Empire, both helping to fund and advise on the war's conduct.

It was an extraordinary adventure, even by his own standards. But, for us, it is his poetry for which he is mainly remembered even though it is difficult to see where he had time to write his works of immense beauty. But write them he did.

He died on April 19th 1824 after having contracted a cold which, on the advice of his doctors, was treated with blood-letting. This caused complications and a violent fever set in. Byron died like his fellow romantics, tragically young and on some foreign field.

Index of Contents
THEATRICAL HISTORY
INTRODUCTION TO WERNER
DEDICATION
PREFACE
DRAMATIS PERSONÆ
MEN
WOMEN
SCENE — Partly on the Frontier of Silesia, and Partly in Siegendorf Castle, near Prague
TIME — The Close of the Thirty Years' War
ACT I
SCENE I. The Hall of a Decayed Palace Stralenheim
ACT II
SCENE I. A Hall in the Same Palace
SCENE II. The Apartment of Werner, in the Palace
ACT III
SCENE I. A Hall in the Same Palace, from Whence the Secret Passage Leads
SCENE II. Stralenheim's Chamber
SCENE III. The Secret Passage
SCENE IV. A Garden
ACT IV
SCENE I. A Gothic Hall in the Castle of Siegendorf, Near Prague
ACT V
SCENE I. A Large and Magnificent Gothic Hall
SCENE II. The Interior of the Turret

NOTE TO THE INTRODUCTION TO WERNER
LORD BYRON – A SHORT BIOGRAPHY
LORD BYRON – A CONCISE BIBLIOGRAPHY

THEATRICAL HISTORY

Werner was produced, for the first time, at the Park Theatre, New York, in 1826. Mr. Barry played "Werner."

Werner was brought out at Drury Lane Theatre, and played, for the first time, December 15, 1830. Macready appeared as "Werner," J. W. Wallack as "Ulric," Mrs. Faucit as "Josephine," and Miss Mordaunt as "Ida." According to the Times, December 16, 1830, "Mr. Macready appeared to very great advantage. We have never seen him exert himself more—we have never known him to exert himself with more powerful effect. Three of his scenes were masterpieces." Genest says that Werner was acted seventeen times in 1830-31.

There was a revival in 1833. Macready says (Diary, March 20) that he acted "'Werner' with unusual force, truth, and collectedness... finished off each burst of passion, and, in consequence, entered on the following emotion with clearness and earnestness" (Macready's Reminiscences, 1875, i 36.6).

Werner was played in 1834, 5, 6, 7, 9; in 1841; in 1843-4 (New York, Boston, Baltimore, New Orleans, Cincinnati, Montreal); in 1845 (Paris, London, Glasgow, Belfast, Dublin); in 1846, 1847; in America in 1848; in the provinces in 1849; in 1850; and, for the last time, at the Theatre Royal, Haymarket, January 14, 1851. At the farewell performance Macready appeared as "Werner," Mr. Davenport as "Ulric," Mrs. Warner as "Josephine," Mrs. Ryder as "Ida." In the same year (1851) a portrait of Macready as "Werner," by Daniel Maclise, R.A., was on view at the Exhibition at the Royal Academy. The motto was taken from Werner, act i. sc. 1, lines 114, sq. (See, for a detailed criticism of Macready's "Werner," Our Recent Actors, by Westland Marston, 1881, i. 89-98; and for the famous "Macready burst," in act ii. sc. 2, and act v. sc. 1, vide ibid., i. 97.)

Werner was brought out at Sadler's Wells Theatre, November 21, 1860, and repeated November 22, 23, 24, 28, 29; December, 3, 4, 11, 13, 14, 1860. Phelps appeared as "Werner," Mr. Edmund Phelps as "Ulric," Miss Atkinson as "Josephine." "Perhaps the old actor never performed the part so finely as he did on that night. The identity between the real and ideal relations of the characters was as vivid to him as to the audience, and gave a deeper intensity, on both sides, to the scenes between father and son." (See The London Stage, by H. Barton Baker, 1889, ii. 217.)

On the afternoon of June 1, 1887, Werner (four acts, arranged by Frank Marshall) was performed at the Lyceum Theatre for the benefit of Westland Marston. Sir Henry Irving appeared as "Werner," Miss Ellen Terry as "Josephine," Mr. Alexander as "Ulric." (See for an appreciation of Sir Henry Irving's presentation of Werner, the Athenæum, June 4, 1887.)]

INTRODUCTION TO WERNER

Werner; or, The Inheritance, was begun at Pisa, December 18, 1821, and finished January 20, 1822. At the end of the month, January 29, Byron despatched the MS., not to Murray, but to Moore, then in retreat at Paris, intending, no doubt, that it should be placed in the hands of another publisher;

but a letter from Murray "melted him," and on March 6, 1822 (Letters, 1901, vi. 34), he desired Moore to forward the packet to Albemarle Street. The play was set up in type, and revised proofs were returned to Murray at the end of June; but, for various reasons, publication was withheld, and, on October 31, Byron informed John Hunt that he had empowered his friend Douglas Kinnaird to obtain Werner, with other MSS., from Murray. None the less, milder counsels again prevailed, and on Saturday, November 23, 1822, Werner was published, not in the same volume with Heaven and Earth, as Byron intended and expected, nor by John Hunt, as he had threatened, but by itself, and, as heretofore, by John Murray. Werner was "the last of all the flock" to issue from Murray's fold.

In his Preface to Werner (vide post, p. 337) Byron disclaims all pretensions to originality. "The following drama," he writes, "is taken entirely from the 'German's Tale, Kruitzner,' published ... in Lee's Canterbury Tales.... I have adopted the characters, plan, and even the language, of many parts of this story." Kruitzner seems to have made a deep impression on his mind. When he was a boy of thirteen (i.e. in 1801, when the fourth volume of the Canterbury Tales was published), and again in 1815, he set himself to turn the tale into a drama. His first attempt, named Ulric and Ilvina, he threw into the fire, but he had nearly completed the first act of his second and maturer adaptation when he was "interrupted by circumstances," that is, no doubt, the circumstances which led up to and ended in the separation from his wife. (See letter of October 9, 1821, Letters, 1901, v. 391.)

On his leaving England for the Continent, April 25, 1816, the fragment was left behind. Most probably the MS. fell into his sister's hands, for in October, 1821, it was not forthcoming when Byron gave directions that Hobhouse should search for it "amongst my papers." Ultimately it came into the possession of the late Mr. Murray, and is now printed for the first time in its entirety (vide post, pp. 453-466: selections were given in the Nineteenth Century, August, 1899). It should be borne in mind that this unprinted first act of Werner, which synchronizes with the Siege of Corinth and Parisina, was written when Byron was a member of the sub-committee of management of Drury Lane Theatre, and, as the numerous stage directions testify, with a view to stage-representation. The MS. is scored with corrections, and betrays an unusual elaboration, and, perhaps, some difficulty and hesitation in the choice of words and the construction of sentences. In the opening scene the situation is not caught and gripped, while the melancholy squalor of the original narrative is only too faithfully reproduced. The Werner of 1821, with all its shortcomings, is the production of a playwright. The Werner of 1815 is the attempt of a highly gifted amateur.

When Byron once more bethought himself of his old subject, he not only sent for the MS. of the first act, but desired Murray "to cut out Sophia Lee's" (vide post, p. 337) "German's Tale from the Canterbury Tales, and send it in a letter" (Letters, 1901, v. 390). He seems to have intended from the first to construct a drama out of the story, and, no doubt, to acknowledge the source of his inspiration. On the whole, he carried out his intention, taking places, characters, and incidents as he found them, but recasting the materials and turning prose into metre. But here and there, to save himself trouble, he "stole his brooms ready made," and, as he acknowledges in the Preface, "adopted even the language of the story." Act ii. sc. 2, lines 87-172; act iii. sc. 4; and act v. sc. 1, lines 94-479, are, more or less, faithful and exact reproductions of pp. 203-206, 228-232, and 252 271 of the novel (see Canterbury Tales, ed. 1832, vol ii.). On the other hand, in the remaining three-fourths of the play, the language is not Miss Lee's, but Byron's, and the "conveyance" of incidents occasional and insignificant. Much, too, was imported into the play (e.g. almost the whole of the fourth act), of which there is neither hint nor suggestion in the story.

Maginn's categorical statement (see "O'Doherty on Werner," Miscellanies, 1885, i. 189) that "here Lord Byron has invented nothing—absolutely, positively, undeniably NOTHING;" that "there is not one incident in his play, not even the most trivial, that is not to be found in the novel," etc., is "positively and undeniably" a falsehood. Maginn read Werner for the purpose of attacking Byron, and, by printing selected passages from the novel and the play, in parallel columns, gives the reader to understand that he had made an exhaustive analysis of the original and the copy. The review, which is quoted as an authority in the editions of 1832 (xiv. pp. 113, 114) and 1837, etc., p. 341, is disingenuous and misleading.

The original story may be briefly retold. The prodigal and outlawed son of a Bohemian noble, Count Siegendorf, after various adventures, marries, under the assumed name of Friedrich Kruitzner, the daughter of an Italian scholar and man of science, of noble birth, but in narrow circumstances. A son, Conrad, is born to him, who, at eight years of age, is transferred to the charge of his grandfather. Twelve years go by, and, when the fortunes of the younger Siegendorf are at their lowest ebb, he learns, at the same moment, that his father is dead, and that a distant kinsman, the Baron Stralenheim, is meditating an attack on his person, with a view to claiming his inheritance. Of Conrad, who has disappeared, he hears nothing.

An accident compels the count and the baron to occupy adjoining quarters in a small town on the northern frontier of Silesia; and, again, another accident places the usurping and intriguing baron at the mercy of his poverty-stricken and exiled kinsman. Stralenheim has fallen asleep near the fire in his easy-chair. Papers and several rouleaux of gold are ranged on a cabinet beside the bed. Kruitzner, who is armed with "a large and sharp knife," is suddenly confronted with his unarmed and slumbering foe, and though habit and conscience conspire to make murder impossible, he yields to a sudden and irresistible impulse, and snatches up "the portion of gold which is nearest." He has no sooner returned to his wife and confessed his deed, than Conrad suddenly appears on the scene, and at the very moment of an unexpected and joyous reunion with his parents, learns that his father is a thief. Kruitzner pleads "guilty with extenuating circumstances," and Conrad, who either is or pretends to be disgusted at his father's sophistries, makes the best of a bad business, and undertakes to conceal his father's dishonour and rescue him from the power of Stralenheim. The plot hinges on the unlooked-for and unsuspected action of Conrad. Unlike his father, he is not the man to let "I dare not wait upon I would," but murders Stralenheim in cold blood, and, at the same time, diverts suspicion from his father and himself to the person of his comrade, a Hungarian soldier of fortune, who is already supposed to be the thief, and who had sought and obtained shelter in the apartments of the conscience-stricken Kruitzner.

The scene changes to Prague. Siegendorf, no longer Kruitzner, has regained his inheritance, and is once more at the height of splendour and prosperity. A service of thanksgiving is being held in the cathedral to commemorate the signature of the Treaty of Prague (1635), and the count is present in state. Suddenly he catches sight of the Hungarian, and, "like a flash of lightning" feels and remembers that he is a thief, and that he might, however unjustly, be suspected if not accused of the murder of Stralenheim. The service is over, and the count is recrossing "Muldau's Bridge," when he hears the fatal word Kruitzner, "the seal of his shame," spoken in his ear. He returns to his castle, and issues orders that the Hungarian should be arrested and interrogated. An interview takes place, at which the Hungarian denounces Conrad as the murderer of Stralenheim. The son acknowledges the deed, and upbraids the father for his weakness and credulity in supposing that his escape from Stralenheim's machinations could have been effected by any other means. If, he argues, circumstances can palliate dishonesty, they can compel and justify murder. Common sense even now demands the immediate slaughter of the Hungarian, as it compelled and sanctioned the effectual silencing of Stralenheim. But Siegendorf knows not "thorough," and shrinks at assassination. He repudiates and denounces his son, and connives at the escape of the Hungarian. Conrad, who is banished from Prague, rejoins his former associates, the "black bands," which were the scandal and terror of the neighbouring provinces, and is killed in a skirmish with the regular troops. Siegendorf dies of a broken heart.

The conception of The German's Tale, as Byron perceived, is superior to the execution. The style is laboured and involved, and the narrative long-winded and tiresome. It is, perhaps, an adaptation, though not a literal translation, of a German historical romance. But the motif—a son predestined to evil by the weakness and sensuality of his father, a father punished for his want of rectitude by the passionate criminality of his son, is the very key-note of tragedy.

If from haste or indolence Byron scamped his task, and cut up whole cantles of the novel into nerveless and pointless blank verse, here and there throughout the play, in scattered lines and passages, he outdoes himself. The inspiration is fitful, but supreme.

Werner was reviewed in Blackwood's Edinburgh Magazine, December, 1822, vol. xii. pp. 710-719 (republished in Miscellanies of W. Maginn, 1885, i. 189); in the Scots Magazine, December, 1822, N.S. vol. xi. pp. 688-694; the European Magazine, January, 1823, vol. 83, pp. 73-76; and in the Eclectic Review, February, 1823, N.S. vol. xix. pp. 148-155.

DEDICATION

TO THE ILLUSTRIOUS GOETHE
BY ONE OF HIS HUMBLEST ADMIRERS,
THIS TRAGEDY IS DEDICATED.

PREFACE

The following drama is taken entirely from the German's Tale, Kruitzner, published many years ago in "Lee's Canterbury Tales" written (I believe) by two sisters, of whom one furnished only this story and another, both of which are considered superior to the remainder of the collection. I have adopted the characters, plan, and even the language of many parts of this story. Some of the characters are modified or altered, a few of the names changed, and one character (Ida of Stralenheim) added by myself: but in the rest the original is chiefly followed. When I was young (about fourteen, I think,) I first read this tale, which made a deep impression upon me; and may, indeed, be said to contain the germ of much that I have since written. I am not sure that it ever was very popular; or, at any rate, its popularity has since been eclipsed by that of other great writers in the same department. But I have generally found that those who had read it, agreed with me in their estimate of the singular power of mind and conception which it developes. I should also add conception, rather than execution; for the story might, perhaps, have been developed with greater advantage. Amongst those whose opinions agreed with mine upon this story, I could mention some very high names: but it is not necessary, nor indeed of any use; for every one must judge according to his own feelings. I merely refer the reader to the original story, that he may see to what extent I have borrowed from it; and am not unwilling that he should find much greater pleasure in perusing it than the drama which is founded upon its contents.

I had begun a drama upon this tale so far back as 1815, (the first I ever attempted, except one at thirteen years old, called "Ulric and Ilvina," which I had sense enough to burn,) and had nearly completed an act, when I was interrupted by circumstances. This is somewhere amongst my papers in England; but as it has not been found, I have re-written the first, and added the subsequent acts.

The whole is neither intended, nor in any shape adapted, for the stage.

DRAMATIS PERSONÆ
MEN
WERNER
ULRIC
STRALENHEIM
IDENSTEIN
GABOR
FRITZ
HENRICK
ERIC
ARNHEIM
MEISTER
RODOLPH
LUDWIG

WOMEN
JOSEPHINE
IDA STRALENHEIM

SCENE — Partly on the Frontier of Silesia, and Partly in Siegendorf Castle, near Prague.

TIME — The Close of the Thirty Years' War

WERNER; OR, THE INHERITANCE

ACT I

SCENE I. The Hall of a Decayed Palace near a Small Town on the Northern Frontier of Silesia—the Night Ttempestuous.

WERNER and JOSEPHINE, his Wife.

JOSEPHINE - My love, be calmer!

WERNER - I am calm.

JOSEPHINE - To me—
Yes, but not to thyself: thy pace is hurried,
And no one walks a chamber like to ours,
With steps like thine, when his heart is at rest.

Were it a garden, I should deem thee happy,
And stepping with the bee from flower to flower;
But here!

WERNER - 'Tis chill; the tapestry lets through
The wind to which it waves: my blood is frozen.

JOSEPHINE - Ah, no!

WERNER - (smiling) Why! wouldst thou have it so?

JOSEPHINE - I would
Have it a healthful current.

WERNER - Let it flow
Until 'tis spilt or checked—how soon, I care not.

JOSEPHINE - And am I nothing in thy heart?

WERNER - All—all.

JOSEPHINE - Then canst thou wish for that which must break mine?

WERNER - (approaching her slowly)
But for thee I had been—no matter what—
But much of good and evil; what I am,
Thou knowest; what I might or should have been,
Thou knowest not: but still I love thee, nor
Shall aught divide us.

[WERNER walks on abruptly, and then approaches JOSEPHINE.

The storm of the night,
Perhaps affects me; I'm a thing of feelings,
And have of late been sickly, as, alas!
Thou know'st by sufferings more than mine, my Love!
In watching me.

JOSEPHINE - To see thee well is much—
To see thee happy—

WERNER - Where hast thou seen such?
Let me be wretched with the rest!

JOSEPHINE - But think
How many in this hour of tempest shiver
Beneath the biting wind and heavy rain,
Whose every drop bows them down nearer earth,
Which hath no chamber for them save beneath
Her surface.

WERNER - And that's not the worst: who cares
For chambers? rest is all. The wretches whom
Thou namest—aye, the wind howls round them, and
The dull and dropping rain saps in their bones
The creeping marrow. I have been a soldier,
A hunter, and a traveller, and am
A beggar, and should know the thing thou talk'st of.

JOSEPHINE - And art thou not now sheltered from them all?

WERNER - Yes. And from these alone.

JOSEPHINE - And that is something.

WERNER - True—to a peasant.

JOSEPHINE - Should the nobly born
Be thankless for that refuge which their habits
Of early delicacy render more
Needful than to the peasant, when the ebb
Of fortune leaves them on the shoals of life?

WERNER - It is not that, thou know'st it is not: we
Have borne all this, I'll not say patiently,
Except in thee—but we have borne it.

JOSEPHINE - Well?

WERNER - Something beyond our outward sufferings (though
These were enough to gnaw into our souls)
Hath stung me oft, and, more than ever, now.
When, but for this untoward sickness, which
Seized me upon this desolate frontier, and
Hath wasted, not alone my strength, but means,
And leaves us—no! this is beyond me!—but
For this I had been happy—thou been happy—
The splendour of my rank sustained—my name—
My father's name—been still upheld; and, more
Than those—

JOSEPHINE - (abruptly) My son—our son—our Ulric,
Been clasped again in these long-empty arms,
And all a mother's hunger satisfied.
Twelve years! he was but eight then:—beautiful
He was, and beautiful he must be now,
My Ulric! my adored!

WERNER - I have been full oft
The chase of Fortune; now she hath o'ertaken
My spirit where it cannot turn at bay,—
Sick, poor, and lonely.

JOSEPHINE - Lonely! my dear husband?

WERNER - Or worse—involving all I love, in this
Far worse than solitude. Alone, I had died,
And all been over in a nameless grave.

JOSEPHINE - And I had not outlived thee; but pray take
Comfort! We have struggled long; and they who strive
With Fortune win or weary her at last,
So that they find the goal or cease to feel
Further. Take comfort,—we shall find our boy.

WERNER - We were in sight of him, of every thing
Which could bring compensation for past sorrow—
And to be baffled thus!

JOSEPHINE - We are not baffled.

WERNER - Are we not penniless?

JOSEPHINE - We ne'er were wealthy.

WERNER - But I was born to wealth, and rank, and power;
Enjoyed them, loved them, and, alas! abused them,
And forfeited them by my father's wrath,
In my o'er-fervent youth: but for the abuse
Long-sufferings have atoned. My father's death
Left the path open, yet not without snares.
This cold and creeping kinsman, who so long
Kept his eye on me, as the snake upon
The fluttering bird, hath ere this time outstept me,
Become the master of my rights, and lord
Of that which lifts him up to princes in
Dominion and domain.

JOSEPHINE - Who knows? our son
May have returned back to his grandsire, and
Even now uphold thy rights for thee?

WERNER - 'Tis hopeless.
Since his strange disappearance from my father's,
Entailing, as it were, my sins upon
Himself, no tidings have revealed his course.
I parted with him to his grandsire, on
The promise that his anger would stop short
Of the third generation; but Heaven seems
To claim her stern prerogative, and visit
Upon my boy his father's faults and follies.

JOSEPHINE - I must hope better still,—at least we have yet

Baffled the long pursuit of Stralenheim.

WERNER - We should have done, but for this fatal sickness;—
More fatal than a mortal malady,
Because it takes not life, but life's sole solace:
Even now I feel my spirit girt about
By the snares of this avaricious fiend:—
How do I know he hath not tracked us here?

JOSEPHINE - He does not know thy person; and his spies,
Who so long watched thee, have been left at Hamburgh.
Our unexpected journey, and this change
Of name, leaves all discovery far behind:
None hold us here for aught save what we seem.

WERNER - Save what we seem! save what we are—sick beggars,
Even to our very hopes.—Ha! ha!

JOSEPHINE - Alas!
That bitter laugh!

WERNER - Who would read in this form
The high soul of the son of a long line?
Who, in this garb, the heir of princely lands?
Who, in this sunken, sickly eye, the pride
Of rank and ancestry? In this worn cheek
And famine-hollowed brow, the Lord of halls
Which daily feast a thousand vassals?

JOSEPHINE - You
Pondered not thus upon these worldly things,
My Werner! when you deigned to choose for bride
The foreign daughter of a wandering exile.

WERNER - An exile's daughter with an outcast son,
Were a fit marriage: but I still had hopes
To lift thee to the state we both were born for.
Your father's house was noble, though decayed;
And worthy by its birth to match with ours.

JOSEPHINE - Your father did not think so, though 'twas noble;
But had my birth been all my claim to match
With thee, I should have deemed it what it is.

WERNER - And what is that in thine eyes?

JOSEPHINE - All which it
Has done in our behalf,—nothing.

WERNER - How,—nothing?

JOSEPHINE - Or worse; for it has been a canker in
Thy heart from the beginning: but for this,
We had not felt our poverty but as
Millions of myriads feel it—cheerfully;
But for these phantoms of thy feudal fathers,
Thou mightst have earned thy bread, as thousands earn it;
Or, if that seem too humble, tried by commerce,
Or other civic means, to amend thy fortunes.

WERNER - (ironically) And been an Hanseatic burgher? Excellent!

JOSEPHINE - Whate'er thou mightest have been, to me thou art
What no state high or low can ever change,
My heart's first choice;—which chose thee, knowing neither
Thy birth, thy hopes, thy pride; nought, save thy sorrows:
While they last, let me comfort or divide them:
When they end—let mine end with them, or thee!

WERNER - My better angel! Such I have ever found thee;
This rashness, or this weakness of my temper,
Ne'er raised a thought to injure thee or thine.
Thou didst not mar my fortunes: my own nature
In youth was such as to unmake an empire,
Had such been my inheritance; but now,
Chastened, subdued, out-worn, and taught to know
Myself,—to lose this for our son and thee!
Trust me, when, in my two-and-twentieth spring,
My father barred me from my father's house,
The last sole scion of a thousand sires
(For I was then the last), it hurt me less
Than to behold my boy and my boy's mother
Excluded in their innocence from what
My faults deserved-exclusion; although then
My passions were all living serpents, and
Twined like the Gorgon's round me.

[A loud knocking is heard.

JOSEPHINE - Hark!

WERNER - A knocking!

JOSEPHINE - Who can it be at this lone hour? We have
Few visitors.

WERNER - And poverty hath none,
Save those who come to make it poorer still.
Well—I am prepared.

[WERNER puts his hand into his bosom, as if to search for some weapon.

JOSEPHINE - Oh! do not look so. I
Will to the door. It cannot be of import
In this lone spot of wintry desolation:—
The very desert saves man from mankind.

[She goes to the door.

Enter IDENSTEIN.

IDENSTEIN - A fair good evening to my fair hostess
And worthy—What's your name, my friend?

WERNER - Are you
Not afraid to demand it?

IDENSTEIN - Not afraid?
Egad! I am afraid. You look as if
I asked for something better than your name,
By the face you put on it.

WERNER - Better, sir!

IDENSTEIN - Better or worse, like matrimony: what
Shall I say more? You have been a guest this month
Here in the prince's palace—(to be sure,
His Highness had resigned it to the ghosts
And rats these twelve years—but 'tis still a palace)—
I say you have been our lodger, and as yet
We do not know your name.

WERNER - My name is Werner.

IDENSTEIN - A goodly name, a very worthy name,
As e'er was gilt upon a trader's board:
I have a cousin in the lazaretto
Of Hamburgh, who has got a wife who bore
The same. He is an officer of trust,
Surgeon's assistant (hoping to be surgeon),
And has done miracles i' the way of business.
Perhaps you are related to my relative?

WERNER - To yours?

JOSEPHINE - Oh, yes; we are, but distantly.
(Aside to WERNER.) Cannot you humour the dull gossip till
We learn his purpose?

IDENSTEIN - Well, I'm glad of that;
I thought so all along, such natural yearnings
Played round my heart:—blood is not water, cousin;
And so let's have some wine, and drink unto

Our better acquaintance: relatives should be
Friends.

WERNER - You appear to have drunk enough already;
And if you have not, I've no wine to offer,
Else it were yours: but this you know, or should know:
You see I am poor, and sick, and will not see
That I would be alone; but to your business!
What brings you here?

IDENSTEIN - Why, what should bring me here?

WERNER - I know not, though I think that I could guess
That which will send you hence.

JOSEPHINE - (aside) Patience, dear Werner!

IDENSTEIN - You don't know what has happened, then?

JOSEPHINE - How should we?

IDENSTEIN - The river has o'erflowed.

JOSEPHINE - Alas! we have known
That to our sorrow for these five days; since
It keeps us here.

IDENSTEIN - But what you don't know is,
That a great personage, who fain would cross
Against the stream and three postilions' wishes,
Is drowned below the ford, with five post-horses,
A monkey, and a mastiff—and a valet.

JOSEPHINE - Poor creatures! are you sure?

IDENSTEIN - Yes, of the monkey,
And the valet, and the cattle; but as yet
We know not if his Excellency's dead
Or no; your noblemen are hard to drown,
As it is fit that men in office should be;
But what is certain is, that he has swallowed
Enough of the Oder to have burst two peasants;
And now a Saxon and Hungarian traveller,
Who, at their proper peril, snatched him from
The whirling river, have sent on to crave
A lodging, or a grave, according as
It may turn out with the live or dead body.

JOSEPHINE - And where will you receive him? here, I hope,
If we can be of service—say the word.

IDENSTEIN - Here? no; but in the Prince's own apartment,
As fits a noble guest:—'tis damp, no doubt,
Not having been inhabited these twelve years;
But then he comes from a much damper place,
So scarcely will catch cold in't, if he be
Still liable to cold—and if not, why
He'll be worse lodged to-morrow: ne'ertheless,
I have ordered fire and all appliances
To be got ready for the worst—that is,
In case he should survive.

JOSEPHINE - Poor gentleman!
I hope he will, with all my heart.

WERNER - Intendant,
Have you not learned his name? (Aside to his wife.) My Josephine,
Retire: I'll sift this fool.

[Exit JOSEPHINE.

IDENSTEIN - His name? oh Lord!
Who knows if he hath now a name or no?
'Tis time enough to ask it when he's able
To give an answer; or if not, to put
His heir's upon his epitaph. Methought
Just now you chid me for demanding names?

WERNER - True, true, I did so: you say well and wisely.

Enter GABOR.

GABOR - If I intrude, I crave—

IDENSTEIN - Oh, no intrusion!
This is the palace; this a stranger like
Yourself; I pray you make yourself at home:
But where's his Excellency? and how fares he?

GABOR - Wetly and wearily, but out of peril:
He paused to change his garments in a cottage
(Where I doffed mine for these, and came on hither),
And has almost recovered from his drenching.
He will be here anon.

IDENSTEIN - What ho, there! bustle!
Without there, Herman, Weilburg, Peter, Conrad!

[Gives directions to different SERVANTS who enter.

A nobleman sleeps here to-night—see that
All is in order in the damask chamber—

Keep up the stove—I will myself to the cellar—
And Madame Idenstein (my consort, stranger,)
Shall furnish forth the bed-apparel; for,
To say the truth, they are marvellous scant of this
Within the palace precincts, since his Highness
Left it some dozen years ago. And then
His Excellency will sup, doubtless?

GABOR - Faith!
I cannot tell; but I should think the pillow
Would please him better than the table, after
His soaking in your river: but for fear
Your viands should be thrown away, I mean
To sup myself, and have a friend without
Who will do honour to your good cheer with
A traveller's appetite.

IDENSTEIN - But are you sure
His Excellency—But his name: what is it?

GABOR - I do not know.

IDENSTEIN - And yet you saved his life.

GABOR - I helped my friend to do so.

IDENSTEIN - Well, that's strange,
To save a man's life whom you do not know.

GABOR - Not so; for there are some I know so well,
I scarce should give myself the trouble.

IDENSTEIN - Pray,
Good friend, and who may you be?

GABOR - By my family,
Hungarian.

IDENSTEIN - Which is called?

GABOR - It matters little.

IDENSTEIN - (aside). I think that all the world are grown anonymous,
Since no one cares to tell me what he's called!
Pray, has his Excellency a large suite?

GABOR - Sufficient.

IDENSTEIN - How many?

GABOR - I did not count them.

We came up by mere accident, and just
In time to drag him through his carriage window.

IDENSTEIN - Well, what would I give to save a great man!
No doubt you'll have a swingeing sum as recompense.

GABOR - Perhaps.

IDENSTEIN - Now, how much do you reckon on?

GABOR - I have not yet put up myself to sale:
In the mean time, my best reward would be
A glass of your Hockcheimer—a green glass,
Wreathed with rich grapes and Bacchanal devices,
O'erflowing with the oldest of your vintage:
For which I promise you, in case you e'er
Run hazard of being drowned, (although I own
It seems, of all deaths, the least likely for you,)
I'll pull you out for nothing. Quick, my friend,
And think, for every bumper I shall quaff,
A wave the less may roll above your head.

IDENSTEIN - (aside) I don't much like this fellow—close and dry
He seems,—two things which suit me not; however,
Wine he shall have; if that unlocks him not,
I shall not sleep to-night for curiosity.

[Exit IDENSTEIN.

GABOR - (to WERNER) This master of the ceremonies is
The intendant of the palace, I presume:
'Tis a fine building, but decayed.

WERNER - The apartment
Designed for him you rescued will be found
In fitter order for a sickly guest.

GABOR - I wonder then you occupied it not,
For you seem delicate in health.

WERNER - (quickly) Sir!

GABOR - Pray
Excuse me: have I said aught to offend you?

WERNER - Nothing: but we are strangers to each other.

GABOR - And that's the reason I would have us less so:
I thought our bustling guest without had said
You were a chance and passing guest, the counterpart
Of me and my companions.

WERNER - Very true.

GABOR - Then, as we never met before, and never,
It may be, may again encounter, why,
I thought to cheer up this old dungeon here
(At least to me) by asking you to share
The fare of my companions and myself.

WERNER - Pray, pardon me; my health—

GABOR - Even as you please.
I have been a soldier, and perhaps am blunt
In bearing.

WERNER - I have also served, and can
Requite a soldier's greeting.

GABOR - In what service?
The Imperial?

WERNER - (quickly, and then interrupting himself).
I commanded—no—I mean
I served; but it is many years ago,
When first Bohemia raised her banner 'gainst
The Austrian.

GABOR - Well, that's over now, and peace
Has turned some thousand gallant hearts adrift
To live as they best may: and, to say truth,
Some take the shortest.

WERNER - What is that?

GABOR - Whate'er
They lay their hands on. All Silesia and
Lusatia's woods are tenanted by bands
Of the late troops, who levy on the country
Their maintenance: the Chatelains must keep
Their castle walls—beyond them 'tis but doubtful
Travel for your rich Count or full-blown Baron.
My comfort is that, wander where I may,
I've little left to lose now.

WERNER - And I—nothing.

GABOR - That's harder still. You say you were a soldier.

WERNER - I was.

GABOR - You look one still. All soldiers are

Or should be comrades, even though enemies.
Our swords when drawn must cross, our engines aim
(While levelled) at each other's hearts; but when
A truce, a peace, or what you will, remits
The steel into its scabbard, and lets sleep
The spark which lights the matchlock, we are brethren.
You are poor and sickly—I am not rich, but healthy;
I want for nothing which I cannot want;
You seem devoid of this—wilt share it?
[GABOR pulls out his purse.

WERNER - Who
Told you I was a beggar?

GABOR - You yourself,
In saying you were a soldier during peace-time.

WERNER - (looking at him with suspicion). You know me not.

GABOR - I know no man, not even
Myself: how should I then know one I ne'er
Beheld till half an hour since?

WERNER - Sir, I thank you.
Your offer's noble were it to a friend,
And not unkind as to an unknown stranger,
Though scarcely prudent; but no less I thank you.
I am a beggar in all save his trade;
And when I beg of any one, it shall be
Of him who was the first to offer what
Few can obtain by asking. Pardon me.

[Exit WERNER.

GABOR - (solus) A goodly fellow by his looks, though worn
As most good fellows are, by pain or pleasure,
Which tear life out of us before our time;
I scarce know which most quickly: but he seems
To have seen better days, as who has not
Who has seen yesterday?—But here approaches
Our sage intendant, with the wine: however,
For the cup's sake I'll bear the cupbearer.

Enter IDENSTEIN.

IDENSTEIN - 'Tis here! the supernaculum! twenty years
Of age, if 'tis a day.

GABOR - Which epoch makes
Young women and old wine; and 'tis great pity,
Of two such excellent things, increase of years,

Which still improves the one, should spoil the other.
Fill full—Here's to our hostess!—your fair wife!

[Takes the glass.

IDENSTEIN - Fair!—Well, I trust your taste in wine is equal
To that you show for beauty; but I pledge you
Nevertheless.

GABOR - Is not the lovely woman
I met in the adjacent hall, who, with
An air, and port, and eye, which would have better
Beseemed this palace in its brightest days
(Though in a garb adapted to its present
Abandonment), returned my salutation—
Is not the same your spouse?

IDENSTEIN - I would she were!
But you're mistaken:—that's the stranger's wife.

GABOR - And by her aspect she might be a Prince's;
Though time hath touched her too, she still retains
Much beauty, and more majesty.

IDENSTEIN - And that
Is more than I can say for Madame Idenstein,
At least in beauty: as for majesty,
She has some of its properties which might
Be spared—but never mind!

GABOR - I don't. But who
May be this stranger? He too hath a bearing
Above his outward fortunes.

IDENSTEIN - There I differ.
He's poor as Job, and not so patient; but
Who he may be, or what, or aught of him,
Except his name (and that I only learned
To-night), I know not.

GABOR - But how came he here?

IDENSTEIN - In a most miserable old caleche,
About a month since, and immediately
Fell sick, almost to death. He should have died.

GABOR - Tender and true!—but why?

IDENSTEIN - Why, what is life
Without a living? He has not a stiver.

GABOR - In that case, I much wonder that a person
Of your apparent prudence should admit
Guests so forlorn into this noble mansion.

IDENSTEIN - That's true: but pity, as you know, does make
One's heart commit these follies; and besides,
They had some valuables left at that time,
Which paid their way up to the present hour;
And so I thought they might as well be lodged
Here as at the small tavern, and I gave them
The run of some of the oldest palace rooms.
They served to air them, at the least as long
As they could pay for firewood.

GABOR - Poor souls!

IDENSTEIN - Aye,
Exceeding poor.

GABOR - And yet unused to poverty,
If I mistake not. Whither were they going?

IDENSTEIN - Oh! Heaven knows where, unless to Heaven itself.
Some days ago that looked the likeliest journey
For Werner.

GABOR - Werner! I have heard the name.
But it may be a feigned one.

IDENSTEIN - Like enough!
But hark! a noise of wheels and voices, and
A blaze of torches from without. As sure
As destiny, his Excellency's come.
I must be at my post; will you not join me,
To help him from his carriage, and present
Your humble duty at the door?

GABOR - I dragged him
From out that carriage when he would have given
His barony or county to repel
The rushing river from his gurgling throat.
He has valets now enough: they stood aloof then,
Shaking their dripping ears upon the shore,
All roaring "Help!" but offering none; and as
For duty (as you call it)—I did mine then,
Now do yours. Hence, and bow and cringe him here!

IDENSTEIN - I cringe!—but I shall lose the opportunity—
Plague take it! he'll be here, and I not there!

[Exit IDENSTEIN hastily.

Re-enter WERNER.

WERNER - (to himself) I heard a noise of wheels and voices. How
All sounds now jar me! [Perceiving GABOR.
Still here! Is he not
A spy of my pursuer's? His frank offer
So suddenly, and to a stranger, wore
The aspect of a secret enemy;
For friends are slow at such.

GABOR - Sir, you seem rapt;
And yet the time is not akin to thought.
These old walls will be noisy soon. The baron,
Or count (or whatsoe'er this half drowned noble
May be), for whom this desolate village and
Its lone inhabitants show more respect
Than did the elements, is come.

IDENSTEIN - (without) This way—
This way, your Excellency:—have a care,
The staircase is a little gloomy, and
Somewhat decayed; but if we had expected
So high a guest—Pray take my arm, my Lord!

Enter STRALENHEIM, IDENSTEIN, and Attendants—partly
his own, and partly Retainers of the Domain of which
IDENSTEIN is Intendant.

STRALENHEIM - I'll rest here a moment.

IDENSTEIN - (to the servants) Ho! a chair!
Instantly, knaves.

[STRALENHEIM sits down.

WERNER - (aside) Tis he!

STRALENHEIM - I'm better now.
Who are these strangers?

IDENSTEIN - Please you, my good Lord,
One says he is no stranger.

WERNER - (aloud and hastily). Who says that?

[They look at him with surprise.

IDENSTEIN - Why, no one spoke of you, or to you!—but
Here's one his Excellency may be pleased
To recognise.

[Pointing to GABOR.

GABOR - I seek not to disturb
His noble memory.

STRALENHEIM - I apprehend
This is one of the strangers to whose aid
I owe my rescue. Is not that the other?

[Pointing to WERNER.

My state when I was succoured must excuse
My uncertainty to whom I owe so much.

IDENSTEIN - He!—no, my Lord! he rather wants for rescue
Than can afford it. 'Tis a poor sick man,
Travel-tired, and lately risen from a bed
From whence he never dreamed to rise.

STRALENHEIM - Methought
That there were two.

GABOR - There were, in company;
But, in the service rendered to your Lordship,
I needs must say but one, and he is absent.
The chief part of whatever aid was rendered
Was his: it was his fortune to be first.
My will was not inferior, but his strength
And youth outstripped me; therefore do not waste
Your thanks on me. I was but a glad second
Unto a nobler principal.

STRALENHEIM - Where is he?

AN ATTENDANT - My Lord, he tarried in the cottage where
Your Excellency rested for an hour,
And said he would be here to-morrow.

STRALENHEIM - Till
That hour arrives, I can but offer thanks,
And then—

GABOR - I seek no more, and scarce deserve
So much. My comrade may speak for himself.

STRALENHEIM - (fixing his eyes upon WERNER: then aside).
It cannot be! and yet he must be looked to.
'Tis twenty years since I beheld him with
These eyes; and, though my agents still have kept
Theirs on him, policy has held aloof

My own from his, not to alarm him into
Suspicion of my plan. Why did I leave
At Hamburgh those who would have made assurance
If this be he or no? I thought, ere now,
To have been lord of Siegendorf, and parted
In haste, though even the elements appear
To fight against me, and this sudden flood
May keep me prisoner here till—

[He pauses and looks at WERNER: then resumes.

This man must
Be watched. If it is he, he is so changed,
His father, rising from his grave again,
Would pass by him unknown. I must be wary:
An error would spoil all.

IDENSTEIN - Your Lordship seems
Pensive. Will it not please you to pass on?

STRALENHEIM - 'Tis past fatigue, which gives my weighed-down spirit
An outward show of thought. I will to rest.

IDENSTEIN - The Prince's chamber is prepared, with all
The very furniture the Prince used when
Last here, in its full splendour.
(Aside). Somewhat tattered,
And devilish damp, but fine enough by torch-light;
And that's enough for your right noble blood
Of twenty quarterings upon a hatchment;
So let their bearer sleep 'neath something like one
Now, as he one day will for ever lie.

STRALENHEIM - (rising and turning to GABOR).
Good night, good people! Sir, I trust to-morrow
Will find me apter to requite your service.
In the meantime I crave your company
A moment in my chamber.

GABOR - I attend you.

STRALENHEIM - (after a few steps, pauses, and calls WERNER)
Friend!

WERNER - Sir!

IDENSTEIN - Sir! Lord—oh Lord! Why don't you say
His Lordship, or his Excellency? Pray,
My Lord, excuse this poor man's want of breeding:
He hath not been accustomed to admission
To such a presence.

STRALENHEIM - (to IDENSTEIN) Peace, intendant!

IDENSTEIN - Oh!
I am dumb.

STRALENHEIM - (to WERNER) Have you been long here?

WERNER - Long?

STRALENHEIM - I sought
An answer, not an echo.

WERNER - You may seek
Both from the walls. I am not used to answer
Those whom I know not.

STRALENHEIM - Indeed! Ne'er the less,
You might reply with courtesy to what
Is asked in kindness.

WERNER - When I know it such
I will requite—that is, reply—in unison.

STRALENHEIM - The intendant said, you had been detained by sickness—
If I could aid you—journeying the same way?

WERNER - (quickly). I am not journeying the same way!

STRALENHEIM - How know ye
That, ere you know my route?

WERNER - Because there is
But one way that the rich and poor must tread
Together. You diverged from that dread path
Some hours ago, and I some days: henceforth
Our roads must lie asunder, though they tend
All to one home.

STRALENHEIM - Your language is above
Your station.

WERNER - (bitterly). Is it?

STRALENHEIM - Or, at least, beyond
Your garb.

WERNER - 'Tis well that it is not beneath it,
As sometimes happens to the better clad.
But, in a word, what would you with me?

STRALENHEIM - (startled) I?

WERNER - Yes—you! You know me not, and question me,
And wonder that I answer not—not knowing
My inquisitor. Explain what you would have,
And then I'll satisfy yourself, or me.

STRALENHEIM - I knew not that you had reasons for reserve.

WERNER - Many have such:—Have you none?

STRALENHEIM - None which can
Interest a mere stranger.

WERNER - Then forgive
The same unknown and humble stranger, if
He wishes to remain so to the man
Who can have nought in common with him.

STRALENHEIM - Sir,
I will not balk your humour, though untoward:
I only meant you service—but good night!
Intendant, show the way! (TO GABOR.) Sir, you will with me?

[Exeunt STRALENHEIM and Attendants; IDENSTEIN and GABOR.

WERNER - (solus). 'Tis he! I am taken in the toils. Before
I quitted Hamburg, Giulio, his late steward,
Informed me, that he had obtained an order
From Brandenburg's elector, for the arrest
Of Kruitzner (such the name I then bore) when
I came upon the frontier; the free city
Alone preserved my freedom—till I left
Its walls—fool that I was to quit them! But
I deemed this humble garb, and route obscure,
Had baffled the slow hounds in their pursuit.
What's to be done? He knows me not by person;
Nor could aught, save the eye of apprehension,
Have recognised him, after twenty years—
We met so rarely and so coldly in
Our youth. But those about him! Now I can
Divine the frankness of the Hungarian, who
No doubt is a mere tool and spy of Stralenheim's,
To sound and to secure me. Without means!
Sick, poor—begirt too with the flooding rivers,
Impassable even to the wealthy, with
All the appliances which purchase modes
Of overpowering peril, with men's lives,—
How can I hope! An hour ago methought
My state beyond despair; and now, 'tis such,
The past seems paradise. Another day,

And I'm detected,—on the very eve
Of honours, rights, and my inheritance,
When a few drops of gold might save me still
In favouring an escape.

Enter IDENSTEIN and FRITZ in conversation.

FRITZ - Immediately.

IDENSTEIN - I tell you, 'tis impossible.

FRITZ - It must
Be tried, however; and if one express
Fail, you must send on others, till the answer
Arrives from Frankfort, from the commandant.

IDENSTEIN - I will do what I can.

FRITZ - And recollect
To spare no trouble; you will be repaid
Tenfold.

IDENSTEIN - The Baron is retired to rest?

FRITZ - He hath thrown himself into an easy chair
Beside the fire, and slumbers; and has ordered
He may not be disturbed until eleven,
When he will take himself to bed.

IDENSTEIN - Before
An hour is past I'll do my best to serve him.

FRITZ - Remember!

[Exit FRITZ.

IDENSTEIN - The devil take these great men! they
Think all things made for them. Now here must I
Rouse up some half a dozen shivering vassals
From their scant pallets, and, at peril of
Their lives, despatch them o'er the river towards
Frankfort. Methinks the Baron's own experience
Some hours ago might teach him fellow-feeling:
But no, "it must" and there's an end. How now?
Are you there, Mynheer Werner?

WERNER - You have left
Your noble guest right quickly.

IDENSTEIN - Yes—he's dozing,
And seems to like that none should sleep besides.

Here is a packet for the Commandant
Of Frankfort, at all risks and all expenses;
But I must not lose time: Good night!

[Exit IDENSTEIN.

WERNER - "To Frankfort!"
So, so, it thickens! Aye, "the Commandant!"
This tallies well with all the prior steps
Of this cool, calculating fiend, who walks
Between me and my father's house. No doubt
He writes for a detachment to convey me
Into some secret fortress.—Sooner than
This—

[WERNER looks around, and snatches up a knife lying on a table in a recess.

Now I am master of myself at least.
Hark,—footsteps! How do I know that Stralenheim
Will wait for even the show of that authority
Which is to overshadow usurpation?
That he suspects me 's certain. I'm alone—
He with a numerous train: I weak—he strong
In gold, in numbers, rank, authority.
I nameless, or involving in my name
Destruction, till I reach my own domain;
He full-blown with his titles, which impose
Still further on these obscure petty burghers
Than they could do elsewhere. Hark! nearer still!
I'll to the secret passage, which communicates
With the—No! all is silent—'twas my fancy!—
Still as the breathless interval between
The flash and thunder:—I must hush my soul
Amidst its perils. Yet I will retire,
To see if still be unexplored the passage
I wot of: it will serve me as a den
Of secrecy for some hours, at the worst.

[WERNER draws a panel, and exit, closing it after him.

Enter GABOR and JOSEPHINE.

GABOR - Where is your husband?

JOSEPHINE - Here, I thought: I left him
Not long since in his chamber. But these rooms
Have many outlets, and he may be gone
To accompany the Intendant.

GABOR - Baron Stralenheim
Put many questions to the Intendant on

The subject of your lord, and, to be plain,
I have my doubts if he means well.

JOSEPHINE - Alas!
What can there be in common with the proud
And wealthy Baron, and the unknown Werner?

GABOR - That you know best.

JOSEPHINE - Or, if it were so, how
Come you to stir yourself in his behalf,
Rather than that of him whose life you saved?

GABOR - I helped to save him, as in peril; but
I did not pledge myself to serve him in
Oppression. I know well these nobles, and
Their thousand modes of trampling on the poor.
I have proved them; and my spirit boils up when
I find them practising against the weak:—
This is my only motive.

JOSEPHINE - It would be
Not easy to persuade my consort of
Your good intentions.

GABOR - Is he so suspicious?

JOSEPHINE - He was not once; but time and troubles have
Made him what you beheld.

GABOR - I'm sorry for it.
Suspicion is a heavy armour, and
With its own weight impedes more than protects.
Good night! I trust to meet with him at day-break.

[Exit GABOR.

Re-enter IDENSTEIN and some Peasants. JOSEPHINE retires up the Hall.

FIRST PEASANT - But if I'm drowned?

IDENSTEIN - Why, you will be well paid for 't,
And have risked more than drowning for as much,
I doubt not.

SECOND PEASANT - But our wives and families?

IDENSTEIN - Cannot be worse off than they are, and may
Be better.

THIRD PEASANT - I have neither, and will venture.

IDENSTEIN - That's right. A gallant carle, and fit to be
A soldier. I'll promote you to the ranks
In the Prince's body-guard—if you succeed:
And you shall have besides, in sparkling coin,
Two thalers.

Third Peasant. No more!

IDENSTEIN - Out upon your avarice!
Can that low vice alloy so much ambition?
I tell thee, fellow, that two thalers in
Small change will subdivide into a treasure.
Do not five hundred thousand heroes daily
Risk lives and souls for the tithe of one thaler?
When had you half the sum?

THIRD PEASANT - Never—but ne'er
The less I must have three.

IDENSTEIN - Have you forgot
Whose vassal you were born, knave?

THIRD PEASANT - No—the Prince's,
And not the stranger's.

IDENSTEIN - Sirrah! in the Prince's
Absence, I am sovereign; and the Baron is
My intimate connection;—"Cousin Idenstein!
(Quoth he) you'll order out a dozen villains."
And so, you villains! troop—march—march, I say;
And if a single dog's ear of this packet
Be sprinkled by the Oder—look to it!
For every page of paper, shall a hide
Of yours be stretched as parchment on a drum,
Like Ziska's skin, to beat alarm to all
Refractory vassals, who can not effect
Impossibilities.—Away, ye earth-worms!

[Exit, driving them out.

JOSEPHINE - (coming forward).
I fain would shun these scenes, too oft repeated,
Of feudal tyranny o'er petty victims;
I cannot aid, and will not witness such.
Even here, in this remote, unnamed, dull spot,
The dimmest in the district's map, exist
The insolence of wealth in poverty
O'er something poorer still—the pride of rank
In servitude, o'er something still more servile;
And vice in misery affecting still

A tattered splendour. What a state of being!
In Tuscany, my own dear sunny land,
Our nobles were but citizens and merchants,
Like Cosmo. We had evils, but not such
As these; and our all-ripe and gushing valleys
Made poverty more cheerful, where each herb
Was in itself a meal, and every vine
Rained, as it were, the beverage which makes glad
The heart of man; and the ne'er unfelt sun
(But rarely clouded, and when clouded, leaving
His warmth behind in memory of his beams)
Makes the worn mantle, and the thin robe, less
Oppressive than an emperor's jewelled purple.
But, here! the despots of the north appear
To imitate the ice-wind of their clime,
Searching the shivering vassal through his rags,
To wring his soul—as the bleak elements
His form. And 'tis to be amongst these sovereigns
My husband pants! and such his pride of birth—
That twenty years of usage, such as no
Father born in a humble state could nerve
His soul to persecute a son withal,
Hath changed no atom of his early nature;
But I, born nobly also, from my father's
Kindness was taught a different lesson. Father!
May thy long-tried and now rewarded spirit
Look down on us and our so long desired
Ulric! I love my son, as thou didst me!
What's that? Thou, Werner! can it be? and thus?

Enter WERNER hastily, with the knife in his hand, by the secret panel, which he closes hurriedly after him.

WERNER - (not at first recognising her).
Discovered! then I'll stab—(recognising her). Ah! Josephine
Why art thou not at rest?

JOSEPHINE - What rest? My God!
What doth this mean?

WERNER - (showing a rouleau).
Here's gold—gold, Josephine,
Will rescue us from this detested dungeon.

JOSEPHINE - And how obtained?—that knife!

WERNER - 'Tis bloodless—yet.
Away—we must to our chamber.

JOSEPHINE - But whence comest thou?

WERNER - Ask not! but let us think where we shall go—
This—this will make us way—(showing the gold)—I'll fit them now.

JOSEPHINE - I dare not think thee guilty of dishonour.

WERNER - Dishonour!

JOSEPHINE - I have said it.

WERNER - Let us hence:
'Tis the last night, I trust, that we need pass here.

JOSEPHINE - And not the worst, I hope.

WERNER - Hope! I make sure.
But let us to our chamber.

JOSEPHINE - Yet one question—
What hast thou done?

WERNER - (fiercely). Left one thing undone, which
Had made all well: let me not think of it!
Away!

JOSEPHINE - Alas that I should doubt of thee!

[Exeunt.

ACT II

SCENE I. A Hall in the Same Palace

Enter IDENSTEIN and Others.

IDENSTEIN - Fine doings! goodly doings! honest doings!
A Baron pillaged in a Prince's palace!
Where, till this hour, such a sin ne'er was heard of.

FRITZ - It hardly could, unless the rats despoiled
The mice of a few shreds of tapestry.

IDENSTEIN - Oh! that I e'er should live to see this day!
The honour of our city's gone for ever.

FRITZ - Well, but now to discover the delinquent:
The Baron is determined not to lose
This sum without a search.

IDENSTEIN - And so am I.

FRITZ - But whom do you suspect?

IDENSTEIN - Suspect! all people
Without—within—above—below—Heaven help me!

FRITZ - Is there no other entrance to the chamber?

IDENSTEIN - None whatsoever.

FRITZ - Are you sure of that?

IDENSTEIN - Certain. I have lived and served here since my birth,
And if there were such, must have heard of such,
Or seen it.

FRITZ - Then it must be some one who
Had access to the antechamber.

IDENSTEIN - Doubtless.

FRITZ - The man called Werner's poor!

IDENSTEIN - Poor as a miser.
But lodged so far off, in the other wing,
By which there's no communication with
The baron's chamber, that it can't be he.
Besides, I bade him "good night" in the hall,
Almost a mile off, and which only leads
To his own apartment, about the same time
When this burglarious, larcenous felony
Appears to have been committed.

FRITZ - There's another,
The stranger—

IDENSTEIN - The Hungarian?

FRITZ - He who helped
To fish the baron from the Oder.

IDENSTEIN - Not
Unlikely. But, hold—might it not have been
One of the suite?

FRITZ - How? We, sir!

IDENSTEIN - No—not you,
But some of the inferior knaves. You say
The Baron was asleep in the great chair—
The velvet chair—in his embroidered night-gown;

His toilet spread before him, and upon it
A cabinet with letters, papers, and
Several rouleaux of gold; of which one only
Has disappeared:—the door unbolted, with
No difficult access to any.

FRITZ - Good sir,
Be not so quick; the honour of the corps
Which forms the Baron's household's unimpeached
From steward to scullion, save in the fair way
Of peculation; such as in accompts,
Weights, measures, larder, cellar, buttery,
Where all men take their prey; as also in
Postage of letters, gathering of rents,
Purveying feasts, and understanding with
The honest trades who furnish noble masters;
But for your petty, picking, downright thievery,
We scorn it as we do board wages. Then
Had one of our folks done it, he would not
Have been so poor a spirit as to hazard
His neck for one rouleau, but have swooped all;
Also the cabinet, if portable.

IDENSTEIN - There is some sense in that—

FRITZ - No, Sir, be sure
'Twas none of our corps; but some petty, trivial
Picker and stealer, without art or genius.
The only question is—Who else could have
Access, save the Hungarian and yourself?

IDENSTEIN - You don't mean me?

FRITZ - No, sir; I honour more
Your talents—

IDENSTEIN - And my principles, I hope.

FRITZ - Of course. But to the point: What's to be done?

IDENSTEIN - Nothing—but there's a good deal to be said.
We'll offer a reward; move heaven and earth,
And the police (though there's none nearer than
Frankfort); post notices in manuscript
(For we've no printer); and set by my clerk
To read them (for few can, save he and I).
We'll send out villains to strip beggars, and
Search empty pockets; also, to arrest
All gipsies, and ill-clothed and sallow people.
Prisoners we'll have at least, if not the culprit;
And for the Baron's gold—if 'tis not found,

At least he shall have the full satisfaction
Of melting twice its substance in the raising
The ghost of this rouleau. Here's alchemy
For your Lord's losses!

FRITZ - He hath found a better.

IDENSTEIN - Where?

FRITZ - In a most immense inheritance.
The late Count Siegendorf, his distant kinsman,
Is dead near Prague, in his castle, and my Lord
Is on his way to take possession.

IDENSTEIN - Was there
No heir?

FRITZ - Oh, yes; but he has disappeared
Long from the world's eye, and, perhaps, the world.
A prodigal son, beneath his father's ban
For the last twenty years; for whom his sire
Refused to kill the fatted calf; and, therefore,
If living, he must chew the husks still. But
The Baron would find means to silence him,
Were he to re-appear: he's politic,
And has much influence with a certain court.

IDENSTEIN - He's fortunate.

FRITZ - 'Tis true, there is a grandson,
Whom the late Count reclaimed from his son's hands,
And educated as his heir; but, then,
His birth is doubtful.

IDENSTEIN - How so?

FRITZ - His sire made
A left-hand, love, imprudent sort of marriage,
With an Italian exile's dark-eyed daughter:
Noble, they say, too; but no match for such
A house as Siegendorf's. The grandsire ill
Could brook the alliance; and could ne'er be brought
To see the parents, though he took the son.

IDENSTEIN - If he's a lad of mettle, he may yet
Dispute your claim, and weave a web that may
Puzzle your Baron to unravel.

FRITZ - Why,
For mettle, he has quite enough: they say,
He forms a happy mixture of his sire

And grandsire's qualities,—impetuous as
The former, and deep as the latter; but
The strangest is, that he too disappeared
Some months ago.

IDENSTEIN - The devil he did!

FRITZ - Why, yes:
It must have been at his suggestion, at
An hour so critical as was the eve
Of the old man's death, whose heart was broken by it.

IDENSTEIN - Was there no cause assigned?

FRITZ - Plenty, no doubt,
And none, perhaps, the true one. Some averred
It was to seek his parents; some because
The old man held his spirit in so strictly
(But that could scarce be, for he doted on him);
A third believed he wished to serve in war,
But, peace being made soon after his departure,
He might have since returned, were that the motive;
A fourth set charitably have surmised,
As there was something strange and mystic in him,
That in the wild exuberance of his nature
He had joined the black bands, who lay waste Lusatia,
The mountains of Bohemia and Silesia,
Since the last years of war had dwindled into
A kind of general condottiero system
Of bandit-warfare; each troop with its chief,
And all against mankind.

IDENSTEIN - That cannot be.
A young heir, bred to wealth and luxury,
To risk his life and honours with disbanded
Soldiers and desperadoes!

FRITZ - Heaven best knows!
But there are human natures so allied
Unto the savage love of enterprise,
That they will seek for peril as a pleasure.
I've heard that nothing can reclaim your Indian,
Or tame the tiger, though their infancy
Were fed on milk and honey. After all,
Your Wallenstein, your Tilly and Gustavus,
Your Bannier, and your Torstenson and Weimar,
Were but the same thing upon a grand scale;
And now that they are gone, and peace proclaimed,
They who would follow the same pastime must
Pursue it on their own account. Here comes
The Baron, and the Saxon stranger, who

Was his chief aid in yesterday's escape,
But did not leave the cottage by the Oder
Until this morning.

Enter STRALENHEIM and ULRIC.

STRALENHEIM - Since you have refused
All compensation, gentle stranger, save
Inadequate thanks, you almost check even them,
Making me feel the worthlessness of words,
And blush at my own barren gratitude,
They seem so niggardly, compared with what
Your courteous courage did in my behalf—

ULRIC - I pray you press the theme no further.

STRALENHEIM - But
Can I not serve you? You are young, and of
That mould which throws out heroes; fair in favour;
Brave, I know, by my living now to say so;
And, doubtlessly, with such a form and heart,
Would look into the fiery eyes of War,
As ardently for glory as you dared
An obscure death to save an unknown stranger,
In an as perilous, but opposite, element.
You are made for the service: I have served;
Have rank by birth and soldiership, and friends,
Who shall be yours. 'Tis true this pause of peace
Favours such views at present scantily;
But 'twill not last, men's spirits are too stirring;
And, after thirty years of conflict, peace
Is but a petty war, as the time shows us
In every forest, or a mere armed truce.
War will reclaim his own; and, in the meantime,
You might obtain a post, which would ensure
A higher soon, and, by my influence, fail not
To rise. I speak of Brandenburgh, wherein
I stand well with the Elector; in Bohemia,
Like you, I am a stranger, and we are now
Upon its frontier.

ULRIC - You perceive my garb
Is Saxon, and, of course, my service due
To my own Sovereign. If I must decline
Your offer, 'tis with the same feeling which
Induced it.

STRALENHEIM - Why, this is mere usury!
I owe my life to you, and you refuse
The acquittance of the interest of the debt,
To heap more obligations on me, till

I bow beneath them.

ULRIC - You shall say so when
I claim the payment.

STRALENHEIM - Well, sir, since you will not—
You are nobly born?

ULRIC - I have heard my kinsmen say so.

STRALENHEIM - Your actions show it. Might I ask your name?

ULRIC - Ulric.

STRALENHEIM - Your house's?

ULRIC - When I'm worthy of it,
I'll answer you.

STRALENHEIM - (aside). Most probably an Austrian,
Whom these unsettled times forbid to boast
His lineage on these wild and dangerous frontiers,
Where the name of his country is abhorred.
[Aloud to FRITZ and IDENSTEIN.
So, sirs! how have ye sped in your researches?

IDENSTEIN - Indifferent well, your Excellency.

STRALENHEIM - Then
I am to deem the plunderer is caught?

IDENSTEIN - Humph!—not exactly.

STRALENHEIM - Or, at least, suspected?

IDENSTEIN - Oh! for that matter, very much suspected.

STRALENHEIM - Who may he be?

IDENSTEIN - Why, don't you know, my Lord?

STRALENHEIM - How should I? I was fast asleep.

IDENSTEIN - And so
Was I—and that's the cause I know no more
Than does your Excellency.

STRALENHEIM - Dolt!

IDENSTEIN - Why, if
Your Lordship, being robbed, don't recognise

The rogue; how should I, not being robbed, identify
The thief among so many? In the crowd,
May it please your Excellency, your thief looks
Exactly like the rest, or rather better:
'Tis only at the bar and in the dungeon,
That wise men know your felon by his features;
But I'll engage, that if seen there but once,
Whether he be found criminal or no,
His face shall be so.

STRALENHEIM - (to FRITZ). Prithee, Fritz, inform me
What hath been done to trace the fellow?

FRITZ - Faith!
My Lord, not much as yet, except conjecture.

STRALENHEIM - Besides the loss (which, I must own, affects me
Just now materially), I needs would find
The villain out of public motives; for
So dexterous a spoiler, who could creep
Through my attendants, and so many peopled
And lighted chambers, on my rest, and snatch
The gold before my scarce-closed eyes, would soon
Leave bare your borough, Sir Intendant!

IDENSTEIN - True;
If there were aught to carry off, my Lord.

ULRIC - What is all this?

STRALENHEIM - You joined us but this morning,
And have not heard that I was robbed last night.

ULRIC - Some rumour of it reached me as I passed
The outer chambers of the palace, but
I know no further.

STRALENHEIM - It is a strange business:
The Intendant can inform you of the facts.

IDENSTEIN - Most willingly. You see—

STRALENHEIM - (impatiently) Defer your tale,
Till certain of the hearer's patience.

IDENSTEIN - That
Can only be approved by proofs. You see—

STRALENHEIM - (again interrupting him, and addressing ULRIC).
In short, I was asleep upon my chair,
My cabinet before me, with some gold

Upon it (more than I much like to lose,
Though in part only): some ingenious person
Contrived to glide through all my own attendants,
Besides those of the place, and bore away
A hundred golden ducats, which to find
I would be fain, and there's an end. Perhaps
You (as I still am rather faint) would add
To yesterday's great obligation, this,
Though slighter, yet not slight, to aid these men
(Who seem but lukewarm) in recovering it?

ULRIC - Most willingly, and without loss of time—
(To IDENSTEIN.) Come hither, mynheer!

IDENSTEIN - But so much haste bodes
Right little speed, and—

ULRIC - Standing motionless
None; so let's march: we'll talk as we go on.

IDENSTEIN - But—

ULRIC - Show the spot, and then I'll answer you.

FRITZ - I will, sir, with his Excellency's leave.

STRALENHEIM - Do so, and take yon old ass with you.

FRITZ - Hence!

ULRIC - Come on, old oracle, expound thy riddle!

[Exit with IDENSTEIN and FRITZ.

STRALENHEIM - (solus) A stalwart, active, soldier-looking stripling,
Handsome as Hercules ere his first labour,
And with a brow of thought beyond his years
When in repose, till his eye kindles up
In answering yours. I wish I could engage him:
I have need of some such spirits near me now,
For this inheritance is worth a struggle.
And though I am not the man to yield without one,
Neither are they who now rise up between me
And my desire. The boy, they say, 's a bold one;
But he hath played the truant in some hour
Of freakish folly, leaving fortune to
Champion his claims. That's well. The father, whom
For years I've tracked, as does the blood-hound, never
In sight, but constantly in scent, had put me
To fault; but here I have him, and that's better.
It must be he! All circumstance proclaims it;

And careless voices, knowing not the cause
Of my enquiries, still confirm it.—Yes!
The man, his bearing, and the mystery
Of his arrival, and the time; the account, too,
The Intendant gave (for I have not beheld her)
Of his wife's dignified but foreign aspect;
Besides the antipathy with which we met,
As snakes and lions shrink back from each other
By secret instinct that both must be foes
Deadly, without being natural prey to either;
All—all—confirm it to my mind. However,
We'll grapple, ne'ertheless. In a few hours
The order comes from Frankfort, if these waters
Rise not the higher (and the weather favours
Their quick abatement), and I'll have him safe
Within a dungeon, where he may avouch
His real estate and name; and there's no harm done,
Should he prove other than I deem. This robbery
(Save for the actual loss) is lucky also;
He's poor, and that's suspicious—he's unknown,
And that's defenceless.—True, we have no proofs
Of guilt—but what hath he of innocence?
Were he a man indifferent to my prospects,
In other bearings, I should rather lay
The inculpation on the Hungarian, who
Hath something which I like not; and alone
Of all around, except the Intendant, and
The Prince's household and my own, had ingress
Familiar to the chamber.

Enter GABOR.

Friend, how fare you?

GABOR - As those who fare well everywhere, when they
Have supped and slumbered, no great matter how—
And you, my Lord?

STRALENHEIM - Better in rest than purse:
Mine inn is like to cost me dear.

GABOR - I heard
Of your late loss; but 'tis a trifle to
One of your order.

STRALENHEIM - You would hardly think so,
Were the loss yours.

GABOR - I never had so much
(At once) in my whole life, and therefore am not
Fit to decide. But I came here to seek you.

Your couriers are turned back—I have outstripped them,
In my return.

STRALENHEIM - You!—Why?

GABOR - I went at daybreak,
To watch for the abatement of the river,
As being anxious to resume my journey.
Your messengers were all checked like myself;
And, seeing the case hopeless, I await
The current's pleasure.

STRALENHEIM - Would the dogs were in it!
Why did they not, at least, attempt the passage?
I ordered this at all risks.

GABOR - Could you order
The Oder to divide, as Moses did
The Red Sea (scarcely redder than the flood
Of the swoln stream), and be obeyed, perhaps
They might have ventured.

STRALENHEIM - I must see to it:
The knaves! the slaves!—but they shall smart for this.

[Exit STRALENHEIM.

GABOR - (solus) There goes my noble, feudal, self-willed Baron!
Epitome of what brave chivalry
The preux Chevaliers of the good old times
Have left us. Yesterday he would have given
His lands (if he hath any), and, still dearer,
His sixteen quarterings, for as much fresh air
As would have filled a bladder, while he lay
Gurgling and foaming half way through the window
Of his o'erset and water-logged conveyance;
And now he storms at half a dozen wretches
Because they love their lives too! Yet, he's right:
'Tis strange they should, when such as he may put them
To hazard at his pleasure. Oh, thou world!
Thou art indeed a melancholy jest!

[Exit GABOR.

SCENE II. The Apartment of Werner, in the Palace

Enter JOSEPHINE and ULRIC.

JOSEPHINE - Stand back, and let me look on thee again!

My Ulric!—my belovéd!—can it be—
After twelve years?

ULRIC - My dearest mother!

JOSEPHINE - Yes!
My dream is realised—how beautiful!—
How more than all I sighed for! Heaven receive
A mother's thanks! a mother's tears of joy!
This is indeed thy work!—At such an hour, too,
He comes not only as a son, but saviour.

ULRIC - If such a joy await me, it must double
What I now feel, and lighten from my heart
A part of the long debt of duty, not
Of love (for that was ne'er withheld)—forgive me!
This long delay was not my fault.

JOSEPHINE - I know it,
But cannot think of sorrow now, and doubt
If I e'er felt it, 'tis so dazzled from
My memory by this oblivious transport!—
My son!

Enter WERNER.

WERNER - What have we here,—more strangers?—

JOSEPHINE - No!
Look upon him! What do you see?

WERNER - A stripling,
For the first time—

ULRIC - (kneeling). For twelve long years, my father!

WERNER - Oh, God!

JOSEPHINE - He faints!

WERNER - No—I am better now—
Ulric! (Embraces him.)

ULRIC - My father, Siegendorf!

WERNER - (starting).   Hush! boy—
The walls may hear that name!

ULRIC - What then?

WERNER - Why, then—

But we will talk of that anon. Remember,
I must be known here but as Werner. Come!
Come to my arms again! Why, thou look'st all
I should have been, and was not. Josephine!
Sure 'tis no father's fondness dazzles me;
But, had I seen that form amid ten thousand
Youth of the choicest, my heart would have chosen
This for my son!

ULRIC - And yet you knew me not!

WERNER - Alas! I have had that upon my soul
Which makes me look on all men with an eye
That only knows the evil at first glance.

ULRIC - My memory served me far more fondly: I
Have not forgotten aught; and oft-times in
The proud and princely halls of—(I'll not name them,
As you say that 'tis perilous)—but i' the pomp
Of your sire's feudal mansion, I looked back
To the Bohemian mountains many a sunset,
And wept to see another day go down
O'er thee and me, with those huge hills between us.
They shall not part us more.

WERNER - I know not that.
Are you aware my father is no more?

ULRIC - Oh, Heavens! I left him in a green old age,
And looking like the oak, worn, but still steady
Amidst the elements, whilst younger trees
Fell fast around him. 'Twas scarce three months since.

WERNER - Why did you leave him?

JOSEPHINE - (embracing ULRIC). Can you ask that question?
Is he not here?

WERNER - True; he hath sought his parents,
And found them; but, oh! how, and in what state!

ULRIC - All shall be bettered. What we have to do
Is to proceed, and to assert our rights,
Or rather yours; for I waive all, unless
Your father has disposed in such a sort
Of his broad lands as to make mine the foremost,
So that I must prefer my claim for form:
But I trust better, and that all is yours.

WERNER - Have you not heard of Stralenheim?

ULRIC - I saved
His life but yesterday: he's here.

WERNER - You saved
The serpent who will sting us all!

ULRIC - You speak
Riddles: what is this Stralenheim to us?

WERNER - Every thing. One who claims our father's lands:
Our distant kinsman, and our nearest foe.

ULRIC - I never heard his name till now. The Count,
Indeed, spoke sometimes of a kinsman, who,
If his own line should fail, might be remotely
Involved in the succession; but his titles
Were never named before me—and what then?
His right must yield to ours.

WERNER - Aye, if at Prague:
But here he is all-powerful; and has spread
Snares for thy father, which, if hitherto
He hath escaped them, is by fortune, not
By favour.

ULRIC - Doth he personally know you?

WERNER - No; but he guesses shrewdly at my person,
As he betrayed last night; and I, perhaps,
But owe my temporary liberty
To his uncertainty.

ULRIC - I think you wrong him
(Excuse me for the phrase); but Stralenheim
Is not what you prejudge him, or, if so,
He owes me something both for past and present.
I saved his life, he therefore trusts in me.
He hath been plundered too, since he came hither:
Is sick, a stranger, and as such not now
Able to trace the villain who hath robbed him:
I have pledged myself to do so; and the business
Which brought me here was chiefly that: but I
Have found, in searching for another's dross,
My own whole treasure—you, my parents!

WERNER - (agitatedly) Who
Taught you to mouth that name of "villain?"

ULRIC - What
More noble name belongs to common thieves?

WERNER - Who taught you thus to brand an unknown being
With an infernal stigma?

ULRIC - My own feelings
Taught me to name a ruffian from his deeds.

WERNER - Who taught you, long-sought and ill-found boy! that
It would be safe for my own son to insult me?

ULRIC - I named a villain. What is there in common
With such a being and my father?

WERNER - Every thing!
That ruffian is thy father!

JOSEPHINE - Oh, my son!
Believe him not—and yet!—(her voice falters.)

ULRIC - (starts, looks earnestly at WERNER and then says slowly)
And you avow it?

WERNER - Ulric, before you dare despise your father,
Learn to divine and judge his actions. Young,
Rash, new to life, and reared in Luxury's lap,
Is it for you to measure Passion's force,
Or Misery's temptation? Wait—(not long,
It cometh like the night, and quickly)—Wait!—
Wait till, like me, your hopes are blighted till
Sorrow and Shame are handmaids of your cabin—
Famine and Poverty your guests at table;
Despair your bed-fellow—then rise, but not
From sleep, and judge! Should that day e'er arrive—
Should you see then the Serpent, who hath coiled
Himself around all that is dear and noble
Of you and yours, lie slumbering in your path,
With but his folds between your steps and happiness,
When he, who lives but to tear from you name,
Lands, life itself, lies at your mercy, with
Chance your conductor—midnight for your mantle—
The bare knife in your hand, and earth asleep,
Even to your deadliest foe; and he as 'twere
Inviting death, by looking like it, while
His death alone can save you:—Thank your God!
If then, like me, content with petty plunder,
You turn aside—I did so.

ULRIC - But—

WERNER - (abruptly) Hear me!
I will not brook a human voice—scarce dare
Listen to my own (if that be human still)—

Hear me! you do not know this man—I do.
He's mean, deceitful, avaricious. You
Deem yourself safe, as young and brave; but learn
None are secure from desperation, few
From subtilty. My worst foe, Stralenheim,
Housed in a Prince's palace, couched within
A Prince's chamber, lay below my knife!
An instant—a mere motion—the least impulse—
Had swept him and all fears of mine from earth.
He was within my power—my knife was raised—
Withdrawn—and I'm in his:—are you not so?
Who tells you that he knows you not? Who says
He hath not lured you here to end you? or
To plunge you, with your parents, in a dungeon?

[He pauses.

ULRIC - Proceed—proceed!

WERNER - Me he hath ever known,
And hunted through each change of time—name—fortune—
And why not you? Are you more versed in men?
He wound snares round me; flung along my path
Reptiles, whom, in my youth, I would have spurned
Even from my presence; but, in spurning now,
Fill only with fresh venom. Will you be
More patient? Ulric!—Ulric!—there are crimes
Made venial by the occasion, and temptations
Which nature cannot master or forbear.

ULRIC - (who looks first at him and then at JOSEPHINE).
My mother!

WERNER - Ah! I thought so: you have now
Only one parent. I have lost alike
Father and son, and stand alone.

ULRIC - But stay!

[WERNER rushes out of the chamber.

JOSEPHINE - (to ULRIC). Follow him not, until this storm of passion
Abates. Think'st thou, that were it well for him,
I had not followed?

ULRIC - I obey you, mother,
Although reluctantly. My first act shall not
Be one of disobedience.

JOSEPHINE - Oh! he is good!
Condemn him not from his own mouth, but trust

To me, who have borne so much with him, and for him,
That this is but the surface of his soul,
And that the depth is rich in better things.

ULRIC - These then are but my father's principles?
My mother thinks not with him?

JOSEPHINE - Nor doth he
Think as he speaks. Alas! long years of grief
Have made him sometimes thus.

ULRIC - Explain to me
More clearly, then, these claims of Stralenheim,
That, when I see the subject in its bearings,
I may prepare to face him, or at least
To extricate you from your present perils.
I pledge myself to accomplish this—but would
I had arrived a few hours sooner!

JOSEPHINE - Aye!
Hadst thou but done so!

Enter GABOR and IDENSTEIN, with Attendants.

GABOR - (to ULRIC). I have sought you, comrade.
So this is my reward!

ULRIC - What do you mean?

GABOR - 'Sdeath! have I lived to these years, and for this!
(To IDENSTEIN.) But for your age and folly, I would—

IDENSTEIN - Help!
Hands off! Touch an Intendant!

GABOR - Do not think
I'll honour you so much as save your throat
From the Ravenstone by choking you myself.

IDENSTEIN - I thank you for the respite: but there are
Those who have greater need of it than me.

ULRIC - Unriddle this vile wrangling, or—

GABOR - At once, then,
The Baron has been robbed, and upon me
This worthy personage has deigned to fix
His kind suspicions—me! whom he ne'er saw
Till yester evening.

IDENSTEIN - Wouldst have me suspect

My own acquaintances? You have to learn
That I keep better company.

GABOR - You shall
Keep the best shortly, and the last for all men,
The worms! You hound of malice!

[GABOR seizes on him.

ULRIC - (interfering) Nay, no violence:
He's old, unarmed—be temperate, Gabor!

GABOR - (letting go IDENSTEIN) True:
I am a fool to lose myself because
Fools deem me knave: it is their homage.

ULRIC - (to IDENSTEIN) How
Fare you?

IDENSTEIN - Help!

ULRIC - I have helped you.

IDENSTEIN - Kill him! then
I'll say so.

GABOR - I am calm—live on!

IDENSTEIN - That's more
Than you shall do, if there be judge or judgment
In Germany. The Baron shall decide!

GABOR - Does he abet you in your accusation?

IDENSTEIN - Does he not?

GABOR - Then next time let him go sink
Ere I go hang for snatching him from drowning.
But here he comes!

Enter STRALENHEIM.

GABOR - (goes up to him). My noble Lord, I'm here!

STRALENHEIM - Well, sir!

GABOR - Have you aught with me?

STRALENHEIM - What should I
Have with you?

GABOR - You know best, if yesterday's
Flood has not washed away your memory;
But that's a trifle. I stand here accused,
In phrases not equivocal, by yon
Intendant, of the pillage of your person
Or chamber:—is the charge your own or his?

STRALENHEIM - I accuse no man.

GABOR - Then you acquit me, Baron?

STRALENHEIM - I know not whom to accuse, or to acquit,
Or scarcely to suspect.

GABOR - But you at least
Should know whom not to suspect. I am insulted—
Oppressed here by these menials, and I look
To you for remedy—teach them their duty!
To look for thieves at home were part of it,
If duly taught; but, in one word, if I
Have an accuser, let it be a man
Worthy to be so of a man like me.
I am your equal.

STRALENHEIM - You!

GABOR - Aye, sir; and, for
Aught that you know, superior; but proceed—
I do not ask for hints, and surmises,
And circumstance, and proof: I know enough
Of what I have done for you, and what you owe me,
To have at least waited your payment rather
Than paid myself, had I been eager of
Your gold. I also know, that were I even
The villain I am deemed, the service rendered
So recently would not permit you to
Pursue me to the death, except through shame,
Such as would leave your scutcheon but a blank.
But this is nothing: I demand of you
Justice upon your unjust servants, and
From your own lips a disavowal of
All sanction of their insolence: thus much
You owe to the unknown, who asks no more,
And never thought to have asked so much.

STRALENHEIM - This tone
May be of innocence.

GABOR - 'Sdeath! who dare doubt it,
Except such villains as ne'er had it?

STRALENHEIM - You
Are hot, sir.

GABOR - Must I turn an icicle
Before the breath of menials, and their master?

STRALENHEIM - Ulric! you know this man; I found him in
Your company.

GABOR - We found you in the Oder;
Would we had left you there!

STRALENHEIM - I give you thanks, sir.

GABOR - I've earned them; but might have earned more from others,
Perchance, if I had left you to your fate.

STRALENHEIM - Ulric! you know this man?

GABOR - No more than you do
If he avouches not my honour.

ULRIC - I
Can vouch your courage, and, as far as my
Own brief connection led me, honour.

STRALENHEIM - Then
I'm satisfied.

GABOR - (ironically). Right easily, methinks.
What is the spell in his asseveration
More than in mine?

STRALENHEIM - I merely said that I
Was satisfied—not that you are absolved.

GABOR - Again! Am I accused or no?

STRALENHEIM - Go to!
You wax too insolent. If circumstance
And general suspicion be against you,
Is the fault mine? Is't not enough that I
Decline all question of your guilt or innocence?

GABOR - My Lord, my Lord, this is mere cozenage,
A vile equivocation; you well know
Your doubts are certainties to all around you—
Your looks a voice—your frowns a sentence; you
Are practising your power on me—because
You have it; but beware! you know not whom
You strive to tread on.

STRALENHEIM - Threat'st thou?

GABOR - Not so much
As you accuse. You hint the basest injury,
And I retort it with an open warning.

STRALENHEIM - As you have said, 'tis true I owe you something,
For which you seem disposed to pay yourself.

GABOR - Not with your gold.

STRALENHEIM - With bootless insolence.

[To his ATTENDANTS and IDENSTEIN.

You need not further to molest this man,
But let him go his way. Ulric, good morrow!

[Exit STRALENHEIM, IDENSTEIN, and Attendants.

GABOR - (following). I'll after him and—

ULRIC - (stopping him) Not a step.

GABOR - Who shall
Oppose me?

ULRIC - Your own reason, with a moment's
Thought.

GABOR - Must I bear this?

ULRIC - Pshaw! we all must bear
The arrogance of something higher than
Ourselves—the highest cannot temper Satan,
Nor the lowest his vicegerents upon earth.
I've seen you brave the elements, and bear
Things which had made this silkworm cast his skin—
And shrink you from a few sharp sneers and words?

GABOR - Must I bear to be deemed a thief? If 'twere
A bandit of the woods, I could have borne it—
There's something daring in it:—but to steal
The moneys of a slumbering man!—

ULRIC - It seems, then,
You are not guilty.

GABOR - Do I hear aright?
You too!

ULRIC - I merely asked a simple question.

GABOR - If the judge asked me, I would answer "No"—
To you I answer thus.

[He draws.

ULRIC - (drawing) With all my heart!

JOSEPHINE - Without there! Ho! help! help!—
Oh, God! here's murder!

[Exit JOSEPHINE, shrieking.

GABOR and ULRIC fight. GABOR is disarmed just as STRALENHEIM, JOSEPHINE, IDENSTEIN, etc., re-enter.

JOSEPHINE - Oh! glorious Heaven! He's safe!

STRALENHEIM - (to JOSEPHINE) Who's safe!

JOSEPHINE - My—

ULRIC - (interrupting her with a stern look, and turning afterwards to STRALENHEIM) Both!
Here's no great harm done.

STRALENHEIM - What hath caused all this?

ULRIC - You, Baron, I believe; but as the effect
Is harmless, let it not disturb you.—Gabor!
There is your sword; and when you bare it next,
Let it not be against your friends.

[ULRIC pronounces the last words slowly and emphatically in a low voice to GABOR.

GABOR - I thank you
Less for my life than for your counsel.

STRALENHEIM - These
Brawls must end here.

GABOR - (taking his sword). They shall. You've wronged me, Ulric,
More with your unkind thoughts than sword: I would
The last were in my bosom rather than
The first in yours. I could have borne yon noble's
Absurd insinuations—ignorance
And dull suspicion are a part of his
Entail will last him longer than his lands—
But I may fit him yet:—you have vanquished me.

I was the fool of passion to conceive
That I could cope with you, whom I had seen
Already proved by greater perils than
Rest in this arm. We may meet by and by,
However—but in friendship.

[Exit GABOR.

STRALENHEIM - I will brook
No more! This outrage following upon his insults,
Perhaps his guilt, has cancelled all the little
I owed him heretofore for the so-vaunted
Aid which he added to your abler succour.
Ulric, you are not hurt?—

ULRIC - Not even by a scratch.

STRALENHEIM - (to IDENSTEIN). Intendant! take your measures to secure
Yon fellow: I revoke my former lenity.
He shall be sent to Frankfort with an escort,
The instant that the waters have abated.

IDENSTEIN - Secure him! He hath got his sword again—
And seems to know the use on't; 'tis his trade,
Belike;—I'm a civilian.

STRALENHEIM - Fool! are not
Yon score of vassals dogging at your heels
Enough to seize a dozen such? Hence! after him!

ULRIC - Baron, I do beseech you!

STRALENHEIM - I must be
Obeyed. No words!

IDENSTEIN - Well, if it must be so—
March, vassals! I'm your leader, and will bring
The rear up: a wise general never should
Expose his precious life—on which all rests.
I like that article of war.

[Exit IDENSTEIN and ATTENDANTS.

STRALENHEIM - Come hither,
Ulric; what does that woman here? Oh! now
I recognise her, 'tis the stranger's wife
Whom they name "Werner."

ULRIC - 'Tis his name.

STRALENHEIM - Indeed!

Is not your husband visible, fair dame?—

JOSEPHINE - Who seeks him?

STRALENHEIM - No one—for the present: but
I fain would parley, Ulric, with yourself
Alone.

ULRIC - I will retire with you.

JOSEPHINE - Not so:
You are the latest stranger, and command
All places here.
(Aside to ULRIC, as she goes out.) O Ulric! have a care—
Remember what depends on a rash word!

ULRIC - (to JOSEPHINE) Fear not!—

[Exit JOSEPHINE.

STRALENHEIM - Ulric, I think that I may trust you;
You saved my life—and acts like these beget
Unbounded confidence.

ULRIC - Say on.

STRALENHEIM - Mysterious
And long-engendered circumstances (not
To be now fully entered on) have made
This man obnoxious—perhaps fatal to me.

ULRIC - Who? Gabor, the Hungarian?

STRALENHEIM - No—this "Werner"—
With the false name and habit.

ULRIC - How can this be?
He is the poorest of the poor—and yellow
Sickness sits caverned in his hollow eye:
The man is helpless.

STRALENHEIM - He is—'tis no matter;—
But if he be the man I deem (and that
He is so, all around us here—and much
That is not here—confirm my apprehension)
He must be made secure ere twelve hours further.

ULRIC - And what have I to do with this?

STRALENHEIM - I have sent
To Frankfort, to the Governor, my friend,

(I have the authority to do so by
An order of the house of Brandenburgh),
For a fit escort—but this curséd flood
Bars all access, and may do for some hours.

ULRIC - It is abating.

STRALENHEIM - That is well.

ULRIC - But how
Am I concerned?

STRALENHEIM - As one who did so much
For me, you cannot be indifferent to
That which is of more import to me than
The life you rescued.—Keep your eye on him!
The man avoids me, knows that I now know him.—
Watch him!—as you would watch the wild boar when
He makes against you in the hunter's gap—
Like him he must be speared.

ULRIC - Why so?

STRALENHEIM - He stands
Between me and a brave inheritance!
Oh! could you see it! But you shall.

ULRIC - I hope so.

STRALENHEIM - It is the richest of the rich Bohemia,
Unscathed by scorching war. It lies so near
The strongest city, Prague, that fire and sword
Have skimmed it lightly: so that now, besides
Its own exuberance, it bears double value
Confronted with whole realms far and near
Made deserts.

ULRIC - You describe it faithfully.

STRALENHEIM - Aye—could you see it, you would say so—but,
As I have said, you shall.

ULRIC - I accept the omen.

STRALENHEIM - Then claim a recompense from it and me,
Such as both may make worthy your acceptance
And services to me and mine for ever.

ULRIC - And this sole, sick, and miserable wretch—
This way-worn stranger—stands between you and
This Paradise?—(As Adam did between

The devil and his)—[Aside].

STRALENHEIM - He doth.

ULRIC - Hath he no right?

STRALENHEIM - Right! none. A disinherited prodigal,
Who for these twenty years disgraced his lineage
In all his acts—but chiefly by his marriage,
And living amidst commerce-fetching burghers,
And dabbling merchants, in a mart of Jews.

ULRIC - He has a wife, then?

STRALENHEIM - You'd be sorry to
Call such your mother. You have seen the woman
He calls his wife.

ULRIC - Is she not so?

STRALENHEIM - No more
Than he's your father:—an Italian girl,
The daughter of a banished man, who lives
On love and poverty with this same Werner.

ULRIC - They are childless, then?

STRALENHEIM - There is or was a bastard,
Whom the old man—the grandsire (as old age
Is ever doting) took to warm his bosom,
As it went chilly downward to the grave:
But the imp stands not in my path—he has fled,
No one knows whither; and if he had not,
His claims alone were too contemptible
To stand.—Why do you smile?

ULRIC - At your vain fears:
A poor man almost in his grasp—a child
Of doubtful birth—can startle a grandee!

STRALENHEIM - All's to be feared, where all is to be gained.

ULRIC - True; and aught done to save or to obtain it.

STRALENHEIM - You have harped the very string next to my heart.
I may depend upon you?

ULRIC - 'Twere too late
To doubt it.

STRALENHEIM - Let no foolish pity shake

Your bosom (for the appearance of the man
Is pitiful)—he is a wretch, as likely
To have robbed me as the fellow more suspected,
Except that circumstance is less against him;
He being lodged far off, and in a chamber
Without approach to mine; and, to say truth,
I think too well of blood allied to mine,
To deem he would descend to such an act:
Besides, he was a soldier, and a brave one
Once—though too rash.

ULRIC - And they, my Lord, we know
By our experience, never plunder till
They knock the brains out first—which makes them heirs,
Not thieves. The dead, who feel nought, can lose nothing,
Nor e'er be robbed: their spoils are a bequest—
No more.

STRALENHEIM - Go to! you are a wag. But say
I may be sure you'll keep an eye on this man,
And let me know his slightest movement towards
Concealment or escape.

ULRIC - You may be sure
You yourself could not watch him more than I
Will be his sentinel.

STRALENHEIM - By this you make me
Yours, and for ever.

ULRIC - Such is my intention.

[Exeunt.

ACT III

SCENE I. A Hall in the Same Palace, from Whence the Secret Passage Leads

Enter WERNER and GABOR.

GABOR - Sir, I have told my tale: if it so please you
To give me refuge for a few hours, well—
If not, I'll try my fortune elsewhere.

WERNER - How
Can I, so wretched, give to Misery
A shelter?—wanting such myself as much
As e'er the hunted deer a covert—

GABOR - Or
The wounded lion his cool cave. Methinks
You rather look like one would turn at bay,
And rip the hunter's entrails.

WERNER - Ah!

GABOR - I care not
If it be so, being much disposed to do
The same myself. But will you shelter me?
I am oppressed like you—and poor like you—
Disgraced—

WERNER - (abruptly). Who told you that I was disgraced?

GABOR - No one; nor did I say you were so: with
Your poverty my likeness ended; but
I said I was so—and would add, with truth,
As undeservedly as you.

WERNER - Again!
As I?

GABOR - Or any other honest man.
What the devil would you have? You don't believe me
Guilty of this base theft?

WERNER - No, no—I cannot.

GABOR - Why that's my heart of honour! yon young gallant—
Your miserly Intendant and dense noble—
All—all suspected me; and why? because
I am the worst clothed, and least named amongst them;
Although, were Momus' lattice in your breasts,
My soul might brook to open it more widely
Than theirs: but thus it is—you poor and helpless—
Both still more than myself.

WERNER - How know you that?

GABOR - You're right: I ask for shelter at the hand
Which I call helpless; if you now deny it,
I were well paid. But you, who seem to have proved
The wholesome bitterness of life, know well,
By sympathy, that all the outspread gold
Of the New World the Spaniard boasts about
Could never tempt the man who knows its worth,
Weighed at its proper value in the balance,
Save in such guise (and there I grant its power,
Because I feel it,) as may leave no nightmare
Upon his heart o' nights.

WERNER - What do you mean?

GABOR - Just what I say; I thought my speech was plain:
You are no thief—nor I—and, as true men,
Should aid each other.

WERNER - It is a damned world, sir.

GABOR - So is the nearest of the two next, as
The priests say (and no doubt they should know best),
Therefore I'll stick by this—as being both
To suffer martyrdom, at least with such
An epitaph as larceny upon my tomb.
It is but a night's lodging which I crave;
To-morrow I will try the waters, as
The dove did—trusting that they have abated.

WERNER - Abated? Is there hope of that?

GABOR - There was
At noontide.

WERNER - Then we may be safe.

GABOR - Are you
In peril?

WERNER - Poverty is ever so.

GABOR - That I know by long practice. Will you not
Promise to make mine less?

WERNER - Your poverty?

GABOR - No—you don't look a leech for that disorder;
I meant my peril only: you've a roof,
And I have none; I merely seek a covert.

WERNER - Rightly; for how should such a wretch as I
Have gold?

GABOR - Scarce honestly, to say the truth on't,
Although I almost wish you had the Baron's.

WERNER - Dare you insinuate?

GABOR - What?

WERNER - Are you aware
To whom you speak?

GABOR - No; and I am not used
Greatly to care. (A noise heard without.) But hark! they come!

WERNER - Who come?

GABOR - The Intendant and his man-hounds after me:
I'd face them—but it were in vain to expect
Justice at hands like theirs. Where shall I go?
But show me any place. I do assure you,
If there be faith in man, I am most guiltless:
Think if it were your own case!

WERNER - (aside) Oh, just God!
Thy hell is not hereafter! Am I dust still?

GABOR - I see you're moved; and it shows well in you:
I may live to requite it.

WERNER - Are you not
A spy of Stralenheim's?

GABOR - Not I! and if
I were, what is there to espy in you?
Although, I recollect, his frequent question
About you and your spouse might lead to some
Suspicion; but you best know—what—and why.
I am his deadliest foe.

WERNER - You?

GABOR - After such
A treatment for the service which in part
I rendered him, I am his enemy:
If you are not his friend you will assist me.

WERNER - I will.

GABOR - But how?

WERNER - (showing the panel). There is a secret spring:
Remember, I discovered it by chance,
And used it but for safety.

GABOR - Open it,
And I will use it for the same.

WERNER - I found it,
As I have said: it leads through winding walls,
(So thick as to bear paths within their ribs,
Yet lose no jot of strength or stateliness,)

And hollow cells, and obscure niches, to
I know not whither; you must not advance:
Give me your word.

GABOR - It is unecessary:
How should I make my way in darkness through
A Gothic labyrinth of unknown windings?

WERNER - Yes, but who knows to what place it may lead?
I know not—(mark you!)—but who knows it might not
Lead even into the chamber of your foe?
So strangely were contrived these galleries
By our Teutonic fathers in old days,
When man built less against the elements
Than his next neighbour. You must not advance
Beyond the two first windings; if you do
(Albeit I never passed them,) I'll not answer
For what you may be led to.

GABOR - But I will.
A thousand thanks!

WERNER - You'll find the spring more obvious
On the other side; and, when you would return,
It yields to the least touch.

GABOR - I'll in—farewell!

[GABOR goes in by the secret panel.

WERNER - (solus) What have I done? Alas! what had I done
Before to make this fearful? Let it be
Still some atonement that I save the man,
Whose sacrifice had saved perhaps my own—
They come! to seek elsewhere what is before them!

Enter IDENSTEIN and Others.

IDENSTEIN - Is he not here? He must have vanished then
Through the dim Gothic glass by pious aid
Of pictured saints upon the red and yellow
Casements, through which the sunset streams like sunrise
On long pearl-coloured beards and crimson crosses.
And gilded crosiers, and crossed arms, and cowls,
And helms, and twisted armour, and long swords,
All the fantastic furniture of windows
Dim with brave knights and holy hermits, whose
Likeness and fame alike rest in some panes
Of crystal, which each rattling wind proclaims
As frail as any other life or glory.
He's gone, however.

WERNER - Whom do you seek?

IDENSTEIN - A villain.

WERNER - Why need you come so far, then?

IDENSTEIN - In the search
Of him who robbed the Baron.

WERNER - Are you sure
You have divined the man?

IDENSTEIN - As sure as you
Stand there: but where's he gone?

WERNER - Who?

IDENSTEIN - He we sought.

WERNER - You see he is not here.

IDENSTEIN - And yet we traced him
Up to this hall. Are you accomplices?
Or deal you in the black art?

WERNER - I deal plainly,
To many men the blackest.

IDENSTEIN - It may be
I have a question or two for yourself
Hereafter; but we must continue now
Our search for t'other.

WERNER - You had best begin
Your inquisition now: I may not be
So patient always.

IDENSTEIN - I should like to know,
In good sooth, if you really are the man
That Stralenheim's in quest of.

WERNER - Insolent!
Said you not that he was not here?

IDENSTEIN - Yes, one;
But there's another whom he tracks more keenly,
And soon, it may be, with authority
Both paramount to his and mine. But come!
Bustle, my boys! we are at fault.

[Exit IDENSTEIN and ATTENDANTS.

WERNER - In what
A maze hath my dim destiny involved me!
And one base sin hath done me less ill than
The leaving undone one far greater. Down,
Thou busy devil, rising in my heart!
Thou art too late! I'll nought to do with blood.

Enter ULRIC.

ULRIC - I sought you, father.

WERNER - Is't not dangerous?

ULRIC - No; Stralenheim is ignorant of all
Or any of the ties between us: more—
He sends me here a spy upon your actions,
Deeming me wholly his.

WERNER - I cannot think it:
'Tis but a snare he winds about us both,
To swoop the sire and son at once.

ULRIC - I cannot
Pause in each petty fear, and stumble at
The doubts that rise like briers in our path,
But must break through them, as an unarmed carle
Would, though with naked limbs, were the wolf rustling
In the same thicket where he hewed for bread.
Nets are for thrushes, eagles are not caught so:
We'll overfly or rend them.

WERNER - Show me how?

ULRIC - Can you not guess?

WERNER - I cannot.

ULRIC - That is strange.
Came the thought ne'er into your mind last night?

WERNER - I understand you not.

ULRIC - Then we shall never
More understand each other. But to change
The topic—

WERNER - You mean to pursue it, as
'Tis of our safety.

ULRIC - Right; I stand corrected.
I see the subject now more clearly, and
Our general situation in its bearings.
The waters are abating; a few hours
Will bring his summoned myrmidons from Frankfort,
When you will be a prisoner, perhaps worse,
And I an outcast, bastardised by practice
Of this same Baron to make way for him.

WERNER - And now your remedy! I thought to escape
By means of this accurséd gold; but now
I dare not use it, show it, scarce look on it.
Methinks it wears upon its face my guilt
For motto, not the mintage of the state;
And, for the sovereign's head, my own begirt
With hissing snakes, which curl around my temples,
And cry to all beholders, Lo! a villain!

ULRIC - You must not use it, at least now; but take
This ring.

[He gives WERNER a jewel.

WERNER - A gem! It was my father's!

ULRIC - And
As such is now your own. With this you must
Bribe the Intendant for his old caleche
And horses to pursue your route at sunrise,
Together with my mother.

WERNER - And leave you,
So lately found, in peril too?

ULRIC - Fear nothing!
The only fear were if we fled together,
For that would make our ties beyond all doubt.
The waters only lie in flood between
This burgh and Frankfort: so far's in our favour
The route on to Bohemia, though encumbered,
Is not impassable; and when you gain
A few hours' start, the difficulties will be
The same to your pursuers. Once beyond
The frontier, and you're safe.

WERNER - My noble boy!

ULRIC - Hush! hush! no transports: we'll indulge in them
In Castle Siegendorf! Display no gold:
Show Idenstein the gem (I know the man,
And have looked through him): it will answer thus

A double purpose. Stralenheim lost gold—
No jewel: therefore it could not be his;
And then the man who was possest of this
Can hardly be suspected of abstracting
The Baron's coin, when he could thus convert
This ring to more than Stralenheim has lost
By his last night's slumber. Be not over timid
In your address, nor yet too arrogant,
And Idenstein will serve you.

WERNER - I will follow
In all things your direction.

ULRIC - I would have
Spared you the trouble; but had I appeared
To take an interest in you, and still more
By dabbling with a jewel in your favour,
All had been known at once.

WERNER - My guardian angel!
This overpays the past. But how wilt thou
Fare in our absence?

ULRIC - Stralenheim knows nothing
Of me as aught of kindred with yourself.
I will but wait a day or two with him
To lull all doubts, and then rejoin my father.

WERNER - To part no more!

ULRIC - I know not that; but at
The least we'll meet again once more.

WERNER - My boy!
My friend! my only child, and sole preserver!
Oh, do not hate me!

ULRIC - Hate my father!

WERNER - Aye,
My father hated me. Why not my son?

ULRIC - Your father knew you not as I do.

WERNER - Scorpions
Are in thy words! Thou know me? in this guise
Thou canst not know me, I am not myself;
Yet (hate me not) I will be soon.

ULRIC - I'll wait!
In the mean time be sure that all a son

Can do for parents shall be done for mine.

WERNER - I see it, and I feel it; yet I feel
Further—that you despise me.

ULRIC - Wherefore should I?

WERNER - Must I repeat my humiliation?

ULRIC - No!
I have fathomed it and you. But let us talk
Of this no more. Or, if it must be ever,
Not now. Your error has redoubled all
The present difficulties of our house
At secret war with that of Stralenheim:
All we have now to think of is to baffle
HIM. I have shown one way.

WERNER - The only one,
And I embrace it, as I did my son,
Who showed himself and father's safety in
One day.

ULRIC - You shall be safe; let that suffice.
Would Stralenheim's appearance in Bohemia
Disturb your right, or mine, if once we were
Admitted to our lands?

WERNER - Assuredly,
Situate as we are now; although the first
Possessor might, as usual, prove the strongest—
Especially the next in blood.

ULRIC - Blood! 'tis
A word of many meanings; in the veins,
And out of them, it is a different thing—
And so it should be, when the same in blood
(As it is called) are aliens to each other,
Like Theban brethren: when a part is bad,
A few spilt ounces purify the rest.

WERNER - I do not apprehend you.

ULRIC - That may be—
And should, perhaps—and yet—but get ye ready;
You and my mother must away to-night.
Here comes the Intendant: sound him with the gem;
'Twill sink into his venal soul like lead
Into the deep, and bring up slime and mud,
And ooze, too, from the bottom, as the lead doth
With its greased understratum; but no less

Will serve to warn our vessels through these shoals.
The freight is rich, so heave the line in time!
Farewell! I scarce have time, but yet your hand,
My father!—

WERNER - Let me embrace thee!

ULRIC - We may be
Observed: subdue your nature to the hour!
Keep off from me as from your foe!

WERNER - Accursed
Be he who is the stifling cause which smothers
The best and sweetest feeling of our hearts;
At such an hour too!

ULRIC - Yes, curse—it will ease you!
Here is the Intendant.

Enter IDENSTEIN.

ULRIC - Master Idenstein,
How fare you in your purpose? Have you caught
The rogue?

IDENSTEIN - No, faith!

ULRIC - Well, there are plenty more:
You may have better luck another chase.
Where is the Baron?

IDENSTEIN - Gone back to his chamber:
And now I think on't, asking after you
With nobly-born impatience.

ULRIC - Your great men
Must be answered on the instant, as the bound
Of the stung steed replies unto the spur:
'Tis well they have horses, too; for if they had not,
I fear that men must draw their chariots, as
They say kings did Sesostris.

IDENSTEIN - Who was he?

ULRIC - An old Bohemian—an imperial gipsy.

IDENSTEIN - A gipsy or Bohemian, 'tis the same,
For they pass by both names. And was he one?

ULRIC - I've heard so; but I must take leave. Intendant,
Your servant!—Werner (to WERNER slightly), if that be your name,

Yours.

[Exit ULRIC.

IDENSTEIN - A well-spoken, pretty-faced young man!
And prettily behaved! He knows his station,
You see, sir: how he gave to each his due
Precedence!

WERNER - I perceived it, and applaud
His just discernment and your own.

IDENSTEIN - That's well—
That's very well. You also know your place, too;
And yet I don't know that I know your place.

WERNER - (showing the ring).
Would this assist your knowledge?

IDENSTEIN - How!—What!—Eh!
A jewel!

WERNER - 'Tis your own on one condition.

IDENSTEIN - Mine!—Name it!

WERNER - That hereafter you permit me
At thrice its value to redeem it: 'tis
A family ring.

IDENSTEIN - A family!—yours!—a gem!
I'm breathless!

WERNER - You must also furnish me,
An hour ere daybreak, with all means to quit
This place.

IDENSTEIN - But is it real? Let me look on it:
Diamond, by all that's glorious!

WERNER - Come, I'll trust you:
You have guessed, no doubt, that I was born above
My present seeming.

IDENSTEIN - I can't say I did,
Though this looks like it: this is the true breeding
Of gentle blood!

WERNER - I have important reasons
For wishing to continue privily
My journey hence.

IDENSTEIN - So then you are the man
Whom Stralenheim's in quest of?

WERNER - I am not;
But being taken for him might conduct
So much embarrassment to me just now,
And to the Baron's self hereafter—'tis
To spare both that I would avoid all bustle.

IDENSTEIN - Be you the man or no, 'tis not my business;
Besides, I never could obtain the half
From this proud, niggardly noble, who would raise
The country for some missing bits of coin,
And never offer a precise reward—
But this!—another look!

WERNER - Gaze on it freely;
At day-dawn it is yours.

IDENSTEIN - Oh, thou sweet sparkler!
Thou more than stone of the philosopher!
Thou touch-stone of Philosophy herself!
Thou bright eye of the Mine! thou loadstar of
The soul! the true magnetic Pole to which
All hearts point duly north, like trembling needles!
Thou flaming Spirit of the Earth! which, sitting
High on the Monarch's Diadem, attractest
More worship than the majesty who sweats
Beneath the crown which makes his head ache, like
Millions of hearts which bleed to lend it lustre!
Shalt thou be mine? I am, methinks, already
A little king, a lucky alchymist!—
A wise magician, who has bound the devil
Without the forfeit of his soul. But come,
Werner, or what else?

WERNER - Call me Werner still;
You may yet know me by a loftier title.

IDENSTEIN - I do believe in thee! thou art the spirit
Of whom I long have dreamed in a low garb.—
But come, I'll serve thee; thou shalt be as free
As air, despite the waters; let us hence:
I'll show thee I am honest—(oh, thou jewel!)
Thou shalt be furnished, Werner, with such means
Of flight, that if thou wert a snail, not birds
Should overtake thee.—Let me gaze again!
I have a foster-brother in the mart
Of Hamburgh skilled in precious stones. How many
Carats may it weigh?—Come, Werner, I will wing thee.

[Exeunt.

SCENE II. Stralenheim's Chamber

STRALENHEIM and FRITZ.

FRITZ - All's ready, my good Lord!

STRALENHEIM - I am not sleepy,
And yet I must to bed: I fain would say
To rest, but something heavy on my spirit,
Too dull for wakefulness, too quick for slumber,
Sits on me as a cloud along the sky,
Which will not let the sunbeams through, nor yet
Descend in rain and end, but spreads itself
'Twixt earth and heaven, like envy between man
And man, an everlasting mist:—I will
Unto my pillow.

FRITZ - May you rest there well!

STRALENHEIM - I feel, and fear, I shall.

FRITZ - And wherefore fear?

STRALENHEIM - I know not why, and therefore do fear more,
Because an undescribable—but 'tis
All folly. Were the locks as I desired
Changed, to-day, of this chamber? for last night's
Adventure makes it needful.

FRITZ - Certainly,
According to your order, and beneath
The inspection of myself and the young Saxon
Who saved your life. I think they call him "Ulric."

STRALENHEIM - You think! you supercilious slave! what right
Have you to tax your memory, which should be
Quick, proud, and happy to retain the name
Of him who saved your master, as a litany
Whose daily repetition marks your duty.—
Get hence; "You think" indeed! you, who stood still
Howling and dripping on the bank, whilst I
Lay dying, and the stranger dashed aside
The roaring torrent, and restored me to
Thank him—and despise you. "You think!" and scarce
Can recollect his name! I will not waste
More words on you. Call me betimes.

FRITZ - Good night!
I trust to-morrow will restore your Lordship
To renovated strength and temper.

[The scene closes.

SCENE III. The Secret Passage

GABOR - (solus) Four—
Five—six hours have I counted, like the guard
Of outposts, on the never-merry clock,
That hollow tongue of time, which, even when
It sounds for joy, takes something from enjoyment
With every clang. 'Tis a perpetual knell,
Though for a marriage-feast it rings: each stroke
Peals for a hope the less; the funeral note
Of Love deep-buried, without resurrection,
In the grave of Possession; while the knoll
Of long-lived parents finds a jovial echo
To triple time in the son's ear. I'm cold—
I'm dark;—I've blown my fingers—numbered o'er
And o'er my steps—and knocked my head against
Some fifty buttresses—and roused the rats
And bats in general insurrection, till
Their curséd pattering feet and whirling wings
Leave me scarce hearing for another sound.
A light! It is at distance (if I can
Measure in darkness distance): but it blinks
As through a crevice or a key-hole, in
The inhibited direction: I must on,
Nevertheless, from curiosity.
A distant lamp-light is an incident
In such a den as this. Pray Heaven it lead me
To nothing that may tempt me! Else—Heaven aid me
To obtain or to escape it! Shining still!
Were it the star of Lucifer himself,
Or he himself girt with its beams, I could
Contain no longer. Softly: mighty well!
That corner's turned—so—ah! no;—right! it draws
Nearer. Here is a darksome angle—so,
That's weathered.—Let me pause.—Suppose it leads
Into some greater danger than that which
I have escaped—no matter, 'tis a new one;
And novel perils, like fresh mistresses,
Wear more magnetic aspects:—I will on,
And be it where it may—I have my dagger
Which may protect me at a pinch.—Burn still,
Thou little light! Thou art my ignis fatuus!

My stationary Will-o'-the-wisp!—So! so!
He hears my invocation, and fails not.

[The scene closes.

SCENE IV. A Garden.

Enter WERNER.

WERNER - I could not sleep—and now the hour's at hand!
All's ready. Idenstein has kept his word;
And stationed in the outskirts of the town,
Upon the forest's edge, the vehicle
Awaits us. Now the dwindling stars begin
To pale in heaven; and for the last time I
Look on these horrible walls. Oh! never, never
Shall I forget them. Here I came most poor,
But not dishonoured: and I leave them with
A stain,—if not upon my name, yet in
My heart!—a never-dying canker-worm,
Which all the coming splendour of the lands,
And rights, and sovereignty of Siegendorf
Can scarcely lull a moment. I must find
Some means of restitution, which would ease
My soul in part: but how, without discovery?—
It must be done, however; and I'll pause
Upon the method the first hour of safety.
The madness of my misery led to this
Base infamy; repentance must retrieve it:
I will have nought of Stralenheim's upon
My spirit, though he would grasp all of mine;
Lands, freedom, life,—and yet he sleeps as soundly
Perhaps, as infancy, with gorgeous curtains
Spread for his canopy, o'er silken pillows,
Such as when—Hark! what noise is that? Again!
The branches shake; and some loose stones have fallen
From yonder terrace.

[ULRIC leaps down from the terrace.

Ulric! ever welcome!
Thrice welcome now! this filial—

ULRIC - Stop! before
We approach, tell me—

WERNER - Why look you so?

ULRIC - Do I

Behold my father, or—

WERNER - What?

ULRIC - An assassin?

WERNER - Insane or insolent!

ULRIC - Reply, sir, as
You prize your life, or mine!

WERNER - To what must I
Answer?

ULRIC - Are you or are you not the assassin
Of Stralenheim?

WERNER - I never was as yet
The murderer of any man. What mean you?

ULRIC - Did not you this night (as the night before)
Retrace the secret passage? Did you not
Again revisit Stralenheim's chamber? and—

[ULRIC pauses.

WERNER - Proceed.

ULRIC - Died he not by your hand?

WERNER - Great God!

ULRIC - You are innocent, then! my father's innocent!
Embrace me! Yes,—your tone—your look—yes, yes,—
Yet say so.

WERNER - If I e'er, in heart or mind,
Conceived deliberately such a thought,
But rather strove to trample back to hell
Such thoughts—if e'er they glared a moment through
The irritation of my oppressed spirit—
May Heaven be shut for ever from my hopes,
As from mine eyes!

ULRIC - But Stralenheim is dead.

WERNER - 'Tis horrible! 'tis hideous, as 'tis hateful!—
But what have I to do with this?

ULRIC - No bolt
Is forced; no violence can be detected,

Save on his body. Part of his own household
Have been alarmed; but as the Intendant is
Absent, I took upon myself the care
Of mustering the police. His chamber has,
Past doubt, been entered secretly. Excuse me,
If nature—

WERNER - Oh, my boy! what unknown woes
Of dark fatality, like clouds, are gathering
Above our house!

ULRIC - My father! I acquit you!
But will the world do so? will even the judge,
If—but you must away this instant.

WERNER - No!
I'll face it. Who shall dare suspect me?

ULRIC - Yet
You had no guests—no visitors—no life
Breathing around you, save my mother's?

WERNER - Ah!
The Hungarian?

ULRIC - He is gone! he disappeared
Ere sunset.

WERNER - No; I hid him in that very
Concealed and fatal gallery.

ULRIC - There I'll find him.

[ULRIC is going.

WERNER - It is too late: he had left the palace ere
I quitted it. I found the secret panel
Open, and the doors which lead from that hall
Which masks it: I but thought he had snatched the silent
And favourable moment to escape
The myrmidons of Idenstein, who were
Dogging him yester-even.

ULRIC - You reclosed
The panel?

WERNER - Yes; and not without reproach
(And inner trembling for the avoided peril)
At his dull heedlessness, in leaving thus
His shelterer's asylum to the risk
Of a discovery.

ULRIC - You are sure you closed it?

WERNER - Certain.

ULRIC - That's well; but had been better, if
You ne'er had turned it to a den for—

[He pauses.

WERNER - Thieves!
Thou wouldst say: I must bear it, and deserve it;
But not—

ULRIC - No, father; do not speak of this:
This is no hour to think of petty crimes,
But to prevent the consequence of great ones.
Why would you shelter this man?

WERNER - Could I shun it?
A man pursued by my chief foe; disgraced
For my own crime: a victim to my safety,
Imploring a few hours' concealment from
The very wretch who was the cause he needed
Such refuge. Had he been a wolf, I could not
Have in such circumstances thrust him forth.

ULRIC - And like the wolf he hath repaid you. But
It is too late to ponder thus:—you must
Set out ere dawn. I will remain here to
Trace the murderer, if 'tis possible.

WERNER - But this my sudden flight will give the Moloch
Suspicion: two new victims in the lieu
Of one, if I remain. The fled Hungarian,
Who seems the culprit, and—

ULRIC - Who seems? Who else
Can be so?

WERNER - Not I, though just now you doubted—
You, my son!—doubted—

ULRIC - And do you doubt of him
The fugitive?

WERNER - Boy! since I fell into
The abyss of crime (though not of such crime), I,
Having seen the innocent oppressed for me,
May doubt even of the guilty's guilt. Your heart
Is free, and quick with virtuous wrath to accuse

Appearances; and views a criminal
In Innocence's shadow, it may be,
Because 'tis dusky.

ULRIC - And if I do so,
What will mankind, who know you not, or knew
But to oppress? You must not stand the hazard.
Away!—I'll make all easy. Idenstein
Will for his own sake and his jewel's hold
His peace—he also is a partner in
Your flight—moreover—

WERNER - Fly! and leave my name
Linked with the Hungarian's, or, preferred as poorest,
To bear the brand of bloodshed?

ULRIC - Pshaw! leave any thing
Except our fathers' sovereignty and castles,
For which you have so long panted, and in vain!
What name? You have no name, since that you bear
Is feigned.

WERNER - Most true: but still I would not have it
Engraved in crimson in men's memories,
Though in this most obscure abode of men—
Besides, the search—

ULRIC - I will provide against
Aught that can touch you. No one knows you here
As heir of Siegendorf: if Idenstein
Suspects, 'tis but suspicion, and he is
A fool: his folly shall have such employment,
Too, that the unknown Werner shall give way
To nearer thoughts of self. The laws (if e'er
Laws reached this village) are all in abeyance
With the late general war of thirty years,
Or crushed, or rising slowly from the dust,
To which the march of armies trampled them.
Stralenheim, although noble, is unheeded
Here, save as such—without lands, influence,
Save what hath perished with him. Few prolong
A week beyond their funeral rites their sway
O'er men, unless by relatives, whose interest
Is roused: such is not here the case; he died
Alone, unknown,—a solitary grave,
Obscure as his deserts, without a scutcheon,
Is all he'll have, or wants. If I discover
The assassin, 'twill be well—if not, believe me,
None else; though all the full-fed train of menials
May howl above his ashes (as they did
Around him in his danger on the Oder),

Will no more stir a finger now than then.
Hence! hence! I must not hear your answer.—Look!
The stars are almost faded, and the grey
Begins to grizzle the black hair of night.
You shall not answer:—Pardon me that I
Am peremptory: 'tis your son that speaks,
Your long-lost, late-found son.—Let's call my mother!
Softly and swiftly step, and leave the rest
To me: I'll answer for the event as far
As regards you, and that is the chief point,
As my first duty, which shall be observed.
We'll meet in Castle Siegendorf—once more
Our banners shall be glorious! Think of that
Alone, and leave all other thoughts to me,
Whose youth may better battle with them—Hence!
And may your age be happy!—I will kiss
My mother once more, then Heaven's speed be with you!

WERNER - This counsel's safe—but is it honourable?

ULRIC - To save a father is a child's chief honour.

[Exeunt.

ACT IV

SCENE I. A Gothic Hall in the Castle of Siegendorf, Near Prague

Enter ERIC and HENRICK, Retainers of the Count.

ERIC - So, better times are come at last; to these
Old walls new masters and high wassail—both
A long desideratum.

HENRICK - Yes, for masters,
It might be unto those who long for novelty,
Though made by a new grave: but, as for wassail,
Methinks the old Count Siegendorf maintained
His feudal hospitality as high
As e'er another Prince of the empire.

ERIC - Why
For the mere cup and trencher, we no doubt
Fared passing well; but as for merriment
And sport, without which salt and sauces season
The cheer but scantily, our sizings were
Even of the narrowest.

HENRICK - The old count loved not

The roar of revel; are you sure that this does?

ERIC - As yet he hath been courteous as he's bounteous,
And we all love him.

HENRICK - His reign is as yet
Hardly a year o'erpast its honeymoon,
And the first year of sovereigns is bridal:
Anon, we shall perceive his real sway
And moods of mind.

ERIC - Pray Heaven he keep the present!
Then his brave son, Count Ulric—there's a knight!
Pity the wars are o'er!

HENRICK - Why so?

ERIC - Look on him!
And answer that yourself.

HENRICK - He's very youthful,
And strong and beautiful as a young tiger.

ERIC - That's not a faithful vassal's likeness.

HENRICK - But
Perhaps a true one.

ERIC - Pity, as I said,
The wars are over: in the hall, who like
Count Ulric for a well-supported pride,
Which awes, but yet offends not? in the field,
Who like him with his spear in hand, when gnashing
His tusks, and ripping up, from right to left,
The howling hounds, the boar makes for the thicket?
Who backs a horse, or bears a hawk, or wears
A sword like him? Whose plume nods knightlier?

HENRICK - No one's, I grant you. Do not fear, if war
Be long in coming, he is of that kind
Will make it for himself, if he hath not
Already done as much.

ERIC - What do you mean?

HENRICK - You can't deny his train of followers
(But few our native fellow-vassals born
On the domain) are such a sort of knaves
As—

[Pauses.

ERIC - What?

HENRICK - The war (you love so much) leaves living.
Like other parents, she spoils her worst children.

ERIC - Nonsense! they are all brave iron-visaged fellows,
Such as old Tilly loved.

HENRICK - And who loved Tilly?
Ask that at Magdebourg—or, for that matter,
Wallenstein either;—they are gone to—

ERIC - Rest!
But what beyond 'tis not ours to pronounce.

HENRICK - I wish they had left us something of their rest:
The country (nominally now at peace)
Is over-run with—God knows who: they fly
By night, and disappear with sunrise; but
Leave us no less desolation, nay, even more,
Than the most open warfare.

ERIC - But Count Ulric—
What has all this to do with him?

HENRICK - With him!
He—might prevent it. As you say he's fond
Of war, why makes he it not on those marauders?

ERIC - You'd better ask himself.

HENRICK - I would as soon
Ask the lion why he laps not milk.

ERIC - And here he comes!

HENRICK - The devil! you'll hold your tongue?

ERIC - Why do you turn so pale?

HENRICK - 'Tis nothing—but
Be silent.

ERIC - I will, upon what you have said.

HENRICK - I assure you I meant nothing,—a mere sport
Of words, no more; besides, had it been otherwise,
He is to espouse the gentle Baroness
Ida of Stralenheim, the late Baron's heiress;
And she, no doubt, will soften whatsoever

Of fierceness the late long intestine wars
Have given all natures, and most unto those
Who were born in them, and bred up upon
The knees of Homicide; sprinkled, as it were,
With blood even at their baptism. Prithee, peace
On all that I have said!

Enter ULRIC and RODOLPH.

Good morrow, count.

ULRIC - Good morrow, worthy Henrick. Eric, is
All ready for the chase?

ERIC - The dogs are ordered
Down to the forest, and the vassals out
To beat the bushes, and the day looks promising.
Shall I call forth your Excellency's suite?
What courser will you please to mount?

ULRIC - The dun,
Walstein.

ERIC - I fear he scarcely has recovered
The toils of Monday: 'twas a noble chase:
You speared four with your own hand.

ULRIC - True, good Eric;
I had forgotten—let it be the grey, then,
Old Ziska: he has not been out this fortnight.

ERIC - He shall be straight caparisoned. How many
Of your immediate retainers shall
Escort you?

ULRIC - I leave that to Weilburgh, our
Master of the horse.

[Exit ERIC.

Rodolph!

RODOLPH - My Lord!

ULRIC - The news
Is awkward from the—

[RODOLPH points to HENRICK.

How now, Henrick? why
Loiter you here?

HENRICK - For your commands, my Lord.

ULRIC - Go to my father, and present my duty,
And learn if he would aught with me before
I mount.

[Exit HENRICK.

Rodolph, our friends have had a check
Upon the frontiers of Franconia, and
'Tis rumoured that the column sent against them
Is to be strengthened. I must join them soon.

RODOLPH - Best wait for further and more sure advices.

ULRIC - I mean it—and indeed it could not well
Have fallen out at a time more opposite
To all my plans.

RODOLPH - It will be difficult
To excuse your absence to the Count your father.

ULRIC - Yes, but the unsettled state of our domain
In high Silesia will permit and cover
My journey. In the mean time, when we are
Engaged in the chase, draw off the eighty men
Whom Wolffe leads—keep the forests on your route:
You know it well?

RODOLPH - As well as on that night
When we—

ULRIC - We will not speak of that until
We can repeat the same with like success:
And when you have joined, give Rosenberg this letter.

[Gives a letter.

Add further, that I have sent this slight addition
To our force with you and Wolffe, as herald of
My coming, though I could but spare them ill
At this time, as my father loves to keep
Full numbers of retainers round the castle,
Until this marriage, and its feasts and fooleries,
Are rung out with its peal of nuptial nonsense.

RODOLPH - I thought you loved the lady Ida?

ULRIC - Why,
I do so—but it follows not from that

I would bind in my youth and glorious years,
So brief and burning, with a lady's zone,
Although 'twere that of Venus:—but I love her,
As woman should be loved—fairly and solely.

RODOLPH - And constantly?

ULRIC - I think so; for I love
Nought else.—But I have not the time to pause
Upon these gewgaws of the heart. Great things
We have to do ere long. Speed! speed! good Rodolph!

RODOLPH - On my return, however, I shall find
The Baroness Ida lost in Countess Siegendorf?

ULRIC - Perhaps: my father wishes it, and, sooth,
'Tis no bad policy: this union with
The last bud of the rival branch at once
Unites the future and destroys the past.

RODOLPH - Adieu.

ULRIC - Yet hold—we had better keep together
Until the chase begins; then draw thou off,
And do as I have said.

RODOLPH - I will. But to
Return—'twas a most kind act in the count
Your father to send up to Konigsberg
For this fair orphan of the Baron, and
To hail her as his daughter.

ULRIC - Wondrous kind!
Especially as little kindness till
Then grew between them.

RODOLPH - The late Baron died
Of a fever, did he not?

ULRIC - How should I know?

RODOLPH - I have heard it whispered there was something strange
About his death—and even the place of it
Is scarcely known.

ULRIC - Some obscure village on
The Saxon or Silesian frontier.

RODOLPH - He
Has left no testament—no farewell words?

ULRIC - I am neither confessor nor notary,
So cannot say.

RODOLPH - Ah! here's the lady Ida.

Enter IDA STRALENHEIM.

ULRIC - You are early, my sweet cousin!

IDA STRALENHEIM - Not too early,
Dear Ulric, if I do not interrupt you.
Why do you call me "Cousin?"

ULRIC - (smiling) Are we not so?

IDA STRALENHEIM - Yes, but I do not like the name; methinks
It sounds so cold, as if you thought upon
Our pedigree, and only weighed our blood.

ULRIC - (starting) Blood!

IDA STRALENHEIM - Why does yours start from your cheeks?

ULRIC - Aye! doth it?

IDA STRALENHEIM - It doth—but no! it rushes like a torrent
Even to your brow again.

ULRIC - (recovering himself). And if it fled,
It only was because your presence sent it
Back to my heart, which beats for you, sweet Cousin!

IDA STRALENHEIM - "Cousin" again.

ULRIC - Nay, then, I'll call you sister.

IDA STRALENHEIM - I like that name still worse.—Would we had ne'er
Been aught of kindred!

ULRIC - (gloomily). Would we never had!

IDA STRALENHEIM - Oh, heavens! and can you wish that?

ULRIC - Dearest Ida!
Did I not echo your own wish?

IDA STRALENHEIM - Yes, Ulric,
But then I wished it not with such a glance,
And scarce knew what I said; but let me be
Sister, or cousin, what you will, so that
I still to you am something.

ULRIC - You shall be
All—all—

IDA STRALENHEIM - And you to me are so already;
But I can wait.

ULRIC - Dear Ida!

IDA STRALENHEIM - Call me Ida,
Your Ida, for I would be yours, none else's—
Indeed I have none else left, since my poor father—

[She pauses.

ULRIC - You have mine—you have me.

IDA STRALENHEIM - Dear Ulric, how I wish
My father could but view my happiness,
Which wants but this!

ULRIC - Indeed!

IDA STRALENHEIM - You would have loved him,
He you; for the brave ever love each other:
His manner was a little cold, his spirit
Proud (as is birth's prerogative); but under
This grave exterior—Would you had known each other!
Had such as you been near him on his journey,
He had not died without a friend to soothe
His last and lonely moments.

ULRIC - Who says that?

IDA STRALENHEIM - What?

ULRIC - That he died alone.

IDA STRALENHEIM - The general rumour,
And disappearance of his servants, who
Have ne'er returned: that fever was most deadly
Which swept them all away.

ULRIC - If they were near him,
He could not die neglected or alone.

IDA STRALENHEIM - Alas! what is a menial to a death-bed,
When the dim eye rolls vainly round for what
It loves?—They say he died of a fever.

ULRIC - Say!

It was so.

IDA STRALENHEIM - I sometimes dream otherwise.

ULRIC - All dreams are false.

IDA STRALENHEIM - And yet I see him as
I see you.

ULRIC - Where?

IDA STRALENHEIM - In sleep—I see him lie
Pale, bleeding, and a man with a raised knife
Beside him.

ULRIC - But you do not see his face?

IDA STRALENHEIM - (looking at him). No! Oh, my God! do you?

ULRIC - Why do you ask?

IDA STRALENHEIM - Because you look as if you saw a murderer!

ULRIC - (agitatedly).
Ida, this is mere childishness; your weakness
Infects me, to my shame: but as all feelings
Of yours are common to me, it affects me.
Prithee, sweet child, change—

IDA STRALENHEIM - Child, indeed! I have
Full fifteen summers!

[A bugle sounds.

RODOLPH - Hark, my Lord, the bugle!

IDA STRALENHEIM - (peevishly to RODOLPH).
Why need you tell him that? Can he not hear it
Without your echo?

RODOLPH - Pardon me, fair Baroness!

IDA STRALENHEIM - I will not pardon you, unless you earn it
By aiding me in my dissuasion of
Count Ulric from the chase to-day.

RODOLPH - You will not,
Lady, need aid of mine.

ULRIC - I must not now
Forgo it.

IDA STRALENHEIM - But you shall!

ULRIC - Shall!

IDA STRALENHEIM - Yes, or be
No true knight.—Come, dear Ulric! yield to me
In this, for this one day: the day looks heavy,
And you are turned so pale and ill.

ULRIC - You jest.

IDA STRALENHEIM - Indeed I do not:—ask of Rodolph.

RODOLPH - Truly,
My Lord, within this quarter of an hour
You have changed more than e'er I saw you change
In years.

ULRIC - 'Tis nothing; but if 'twere, the air
Would soon restore me. I'm the true cameleon,
And live but on the atmosphere; your feasts
In castle halls, and social banquets, nurse not
My spirit—I'm a forester and breather
Of the steep mountain-tops, where I love all
The eagle loves.

IDA STRALENHEIM - Except his prey, I hope.

ULRIC - Sweet Ida, wish me a fair chase, and I
Will bring you six boars' heads for trophies home.

IDA STRALENHEIM - And will you not stay, then? You shall not go!
Come! I will sing to you.

ULRIC - Ida, you scarcely
Will make a soldier's wife.

IDA STRALENHEIM - I do not wish
To be so; for I trust these wars are over,
And you will live in peace on your domains.

Enter WERNER as COUNT SIEGENDORF.

ULRIC - My father, I salute you, and it grieves me
With such brief greeting.—You have heard our bugle;
The vassals wait.

COUNT SIEGENDORF - So let them.—You forget
To-morrow is the appointed festival
In Prague for peace restored. You are apt to follow

The chase with such an ardour as will scarce
Permit you to return to-day, or if
Returned, too much fatigued to join to-morrow
The nobles in our marshalled ranks.

ULRIC - You, Count,
Will well supply the place of both—I am not
A lover of these pageantries.

COUNT SIEGENDORF - No, Ulric;
It were not well that you alone of all
Our young nobility—

IDA STRALENHEIM - And far the noblest
In aspect and demeanour.

COUNT SIEGENDORF - (to IDA) True, dear child,
Though somewhat frankly said for a fair damsel.—
But, Ulric, recollect too our position,
So lately reinstated in our honours.
Believe me, 'twould be marked in any house,
But most in ours, that ONE should be found wanting
At such a time and place. Besides, the Heaven
Which gave us back our own, in the same moment
It spread its peace o'er all, hath double claims
On us for thanksgiving: first, for our country;
And next, that we are here to share its blessings.

ULRIC - (aside). Devout, too! Well, sir, I obey at once.

(Then aloud to a SERVANT)

Ludwig, dismiss the train without!

[Exit LUDWIG.

IDA STRALENHEIM - And so
You yield, at once, to him what I for hours
Might supplicate in vain.

COUNT SIEGENDORF - (smiling) You are not jealous
Of me, I trust, my pretty rebel! who
Would sanction disobedience against all
Except thyself? But fear not; thou shalt rule him
Hereafter with a fonder sway and firmer.

IDA STRALENHEIM - But I should like to govern now.

COUNT SIEGENDORF - You shall,
Your harp, which by the way awaits you with
The Countess in her chamber. She complains

That you are a sad truant to your music:
She attends you.

IDA STRALENHEIM - Then good morrow, my kind kinsmen!
Ulric, you'll come and hear me?

ULRIC - By and by.

IDA STRALENHEIM - Be sure I'll sound it better than your bugles;
Then pray you be as punctual to its notes:
I'll play you King Gustavus' march.

ULRIC - And why not
Old Tilly's?

IDA STRALENHEIM - Not that monster's! I should think
My harp-strings rang with groans, and not with music,
Could aught of his sound on it:—but come quickly;
Your mother will be eager to receive you.

[Exit IDA.

COUNT SIEGENDORF - Ulric, I wish to speak with you alone.

ULRIC - My time's your vassal.—
(Aside to RODOLPH.) Rodolph, hence! and do
As I directed: and by his best speed
And readiest means let Rosenberg reply.

RODOLPH - Count Siegendorf, command you aught? I am bound
Upon a journey past the frontier.

COUNT SIEGENDORF - (starts) Ah!—
Where? on what frontier?

RODOLPH - The Silesian, on
My way—(Aside to ULRIC.)—Where shall I say?

ULRIC - (aside to RODOLPH) To Hamburgh.
(Aside to himself). That
Word will, I think, put a firm padlock on
His further inquisition.

RODOLPH - Count, to Hamburgh.

COUNT SIEGENDORF - (agitated). Hamburgh! No, I have nought to do there, nor
Am aught connected with that city. Then
God speed you!

RODOLPH - Fare ye well, Count Siegendorf!

[Exit RODOLPH.

COUNT SIEGENDORF - Ulric, this man, who has just departed, is
One of those strange companions whom I fain
Would reason with you on.

ULRIC - My Lord, he is
Noble by birth, of one of the first houses
In Saxony.

COUNT SIEGENDORF - I talk not of his birth,
But of his bearing. Men speak lightly of him.

ULRIC - So they will do of most men. Even the monarch
Is not fenced from his chamberlain's slander, or
The sneer of the last courtier whom he has made
Great and ungrateful.

COUNT SIEGENDORF - If I must be plain,
The world speaks more than lightly of this Rodolph:
They say he is leagued with the "black bands" who still
Ravage the frontier.

ULRIC - And will you believe
The world?

COUNT SIEGENDORF - In this case—yes.

ULRIC - In any case,
I thought you knew it better than to take
An accusation for a sentence.

COUNT SIEGENDORF - Son!
I understand you: you refer to—but
My destiny has so involved about me
Her spider web, that I can only flutter
Like the poor fly, but break it not. Take heed,
Ulric; you have seen to what the passions led me:
Twenty long years of misery and famine
Quenched them not—twenty thousand more, perchance,
Hereafter (or even here in moments which
Might date for years, did Anguish make the dial),
May not obliterate or expiate
The madness and dishonour of an instant.
Ulric, be warned by a father!—I was not
By mine, and you behold me!

ULRIC - I behold
The prosperous and belovéd Siegendorf,
Lord of a Prince's appanage, and honoured
By those he rules and those he ranks with.

COUNT SIEGENDORF - Ah!
Why wilt thou call me prosperous, while I fear
For thee? Belovéd, when thou lovest me not!
All hearts but one may beat in kindness for me—
But if my son's is cold!—

ULRIC - Who dare say that?

COUNT SIEGENDORF - None else but I, who see it—feel it—keener
Than would your adversary, who dared say so,
Your sabre in his heart! But mine survives
The wound.

ULRIC - You err. My nature is not given
To outward fondling: how should it be so,
After twelve years' divorcement from my parents?

COUNT SIEGENDORF - And did not I too pass those twelve torn years
In a like absence? But 'tis vain to urge you—
Nature was never called back by remonstrance.
Let's change the theme. I wish you to consider
That these young violent nobles of high name,
But dark deeds (aye, the darkest, if all Rumour
Reports be true), with whom thou consortest,
Will lead thee—

ULRIC - (impatiently). I'll be led by no man.

COUNT SIEGENDORF - Nor
Be leader of such, I would hope: at once
To wean thee from the perils of thy youth
And haughty spirit, I have thought it well
That thou shouldst wed the lady Ida—more
As thou appear'st to love her.

ULRIC - I have said
I will obey your orders, were they to
Unite with Hecate—can a son say more?

COUNT SIEGENDORF - He says too much in saying this. It is not
The nature of thine age, nor of thy blood,
Nor of thy temperament, to talk so coolly,
Or act so carelessly, in that which is
The bloom or blight of all men's happiness,
(For Glory's pillow is but restless, if
Love lay not down his cheek there): some strong bias,
Some master fiend is in thy service, to
Misrule the mortal who believes him slave,
And makes his every thought subservient; else
Thou'dst say at once—"I love young Ida, and

Will wed her;" or, "I love her not, and all
The powers on earth shall never make me."—So
Would I have answered.

ULRIC - Sir, you wed for love.

COUNT SIEGENDORF - I did, and it has been my only refuge
In many miseries.

ULRIC - Which miseries
Had never been but for this love-match.

COUNT SIEGENDORF - Still
Against your age and nature! Who at twenty
E'er answered thus till now?

ULRIC - Did you not warn me
Against your own example?

COUNT SIEGENDORF - Boyish sophist!
In a word, do you love, or love not, Ida?

ULRIC - What matters it, if I am ready to
Obey you in espousing her?

COUNT SIEGENDORF - As far
As you feel, nothing—but all life for her.
She's young—all-beautiful—adores you—is
Endowed with qualities to give happiness,
Such as rounds common life into a dream
Of something which your poets cannot paint,
And (if it were not wisdom to love virtue),
For which Philosophy might barter Wisdom;
And giving so much happiness, deserves
A little in return. I would not have her
Break her heart with a man who has none to break!
Or wither on her stalk like some pale rose
Deserted by the bird she thought a nightingale,
According to the Orient tale. She is—

ULRIC - The daughter of dead Stralenheim, your foe:
I'll wed her, ne'ertheless; though, to say truth,
Just now I am not violently transported
In favour of such unions.

COUNT SIEGENDORF - But she loves you.

ULRIC - And I love her, and therefore would think twice.

COUNT SIEGENDORF - Alas! Love never did so.

ULRIC - Then 'tis time
He should begin, and take the bandage from
His eyes, and look before he leaps; till now
He hath ta'en a jump i' the dark.

COUNT SIEGENDORF - But you consent?

ULRIC - I did, and do.

COUNT SIEGENDORF - Then fix the day.

ULRIC - Tis usual,
And, certes, courteous, to leave that to the lady.

COUNT SIEGENDORF - I will engage for her.

ULRIC - So will not I
For any woman: and as what I fix,
I fain would see unshaken, when she gives
Her answer, I'll give mine.

COUNT SIEGENDORF - But 'tis your office
To woo.

ULRIC - Count, 'tis a marriage of your making,
So be it of your wooing; but to please you,
I will now pay my duty to my mother,
With whom, you know, the lady Ida is.—
What would you have? You have forbid my stirring
For manly sports beyond the castle walls,
And I obey; you bid me turn a chamberer,
To pick up gloves, and fans, and knitting-needles,
And list to songs and tunes, and watch for smiles,
And smile at pretty prattle, and look into
The eyes of feminine, as though they were
The stars receding early to our wish
Upon the dawn of a world-winning battle—
What can a son or man do more?

[Exit ULRIC.

COUNT SIEGENDORF - (solus) Too much!—
Too much of duty, and too little love!
He pays me in the coin he owes me not:
For such hath been my wayward fate, I could not
Fulfil a parent's duties by his side
Till now; but love he owes me, for my thoughts
Ne'er left him, nor my eyes longed without tears
To see my child again,—and now I have found him!
But how! obedient, but with coldness; duteous
In my sight, but with carelessness; mysterious—

Abstracted—distant—much given to long absence,
And where—none know—in league with the most riotous
Of our young nobles; though, to do him justice,
He never stoops down to their vulgar pleasures;
Yet there's some tie between them which I can not
Unravel. They look up to him—consult him—
Throng round him as a leader: but with me
He hath no confidence! Ah! can I hope it
After—what! doth my father's curse descend
Even to my child? Or is the Hungarian near
To shed more blood? or—Oh! if it should be!
Spirit of Stralenheim, dost thou walk these walls
To wither him and his—who, though they slew not,
Unlatched the door of Death for thee? 'Twas not
Our fault, nor is our sin: thou wert our foe,
And yet I spared thee when my own destruction
Slept with thee, to awake with thine awakening!
And only took—Accurséd gold! thou liest
Like poison in my hands; I dare not use thee,
Nor part from thee; thou camest in such a guise,
Methinks thou wouldst contaminate all hands
Like mine. Yet I have done, to atone for thee,
Thou villanous gold! and thy dead master's doom,
Though he died not by me or mine, as much
As if he were my brother! I have ta'en
His orphan Ida—cherished her as one
Who will be mine.

Enter an ATTENDANT.

ATTENDANT - The abbot, if it please
Your Excellency, whom you sent for, waits
Upon you.

[Exit ATTENDANT.

Enter the PRIOR ALBERT.

PRIOR ALBERT - Peace be with these walls, and all
Within them!

COUNT SIEGENDORF - Welcome, welcome, holy father!
And may thy prayer be heard!—all men have need
Of such, and I—

PRIOR ALBERT - Have the first claim to all
The prayers of our community. Our convent,
Erected by your ancestors, is still
Protected by their children.

COUNT SIEGENDORF - Yes, good father;

Continue daily orisons for us
In these dim days of heresies and blood,
Though the schismatic Swede, Gustavus, is
Gone home.

PRIOR ALBERT - To the endless home of unbelievers,
Where there is everlasting wail and woe,
Gnashing of teeth, and tears of blood, and fire
Eternal and the worm which dieth not!

COUNT SIEGENDORF - True, father: and to avert those pangs from one,
Who, though of our most faultless holy Church,
Yet died without its last and dearest offices,
Which smooth the soul through purgatorial pains,
I have to offer humbly this donation
In masses for his spirit.

[SIEGENDORF offers the gold which he had taken from STRALENHEIM.

PRIOR ALBERT - Count, if I
Receive it, 'tis because I know too well
Refusal would offend you. Be assured
The largess shall be only dealt in alms,
And every mass no less sung for the dead.
Our House needs no donations, thanks to yours,
Which has of old endowed it; but from you
And yours in all meet things 'tis fit we obey.
For whom shall mass be said?

COUNT SIEGENDORF - (faltering) For—for—the dead.

PRIOR ALBERT - His name?

COUNT SIEGENDORF - 'Tis from a soul, and not a name,
I would avert perdition.

PRIOR ALBERT - I meant not
To pry into your secret. We will pray
For one unknown, the same as for the proudest.

COUNT SIEGENDORF - Secret! I have none: but, father, he who's gone
Might have one; or, in short, he did bequeath—
No, not bequeath—but I bestow this sum
For pious purposes.

PRIOR ALBERT - A proper deed
In the behalf of our departed friends.

COUNT SIEGENDORF - But he who's gone was not my friend, but foe,
The deadliest and the stanchest.

PRIOR ALBERT - Better still!
To employ our means to obtain Heaven for the souls
Of our dead enemies is worthy those
Who can forgive them living.

COUNT SIEGENDORF - But I did not
Forgive this man. I loathed him to the last,
As he did me. I do not love him now,
But—

PRIOR ALBERT - Best of all! for this is pure religion!
You fain would rescue him you hate from hell—
An evangelical compassion—with
Your own gold too!

COUNT SIEGENDORF - Father, 'tis not my gold.

PRIOR ALBERT - Whose, then? You said it was no legacy.

COUNT SIEGENDORF - No matter whose—of this be sure, that he
Who owned it never more will need it, save
In that which it may purchase from your altars:
'Tis yours, or theirs.

PRIOR ALBERT - Is there no blood upon it?

COUNT SIEGENDORF - No; but there's worse than blood—eternal shame!

PRIOR ALBERT - Did he who owned it die in his bed?

COUNT SIEGENDORF - Alas!
He did.

PRIOR ALBERT - Son! you relapse into revenge,
If you regret your enemy's bloodless death.

COUNT SIEGENDORF - His death was fathomlessly deep in blood.

PRIOR ALBERT - You said he died in his bed, not battle.

COUNT SIEGENDORF - He
Died, I scarce know—but—he was stabbed i' the dark,
And now you have it—perished on his pillow
By a cut-throat!—Aye!—you may look upon me!
I am not the man. I'll meet your eye on that point,
As I can one day God's.

PRIOR ALBERT - Nor did he die
By means, or men, or instrument of yours?

COUNT SIEGENDORF - No! by the God who sees and strikes!

PRIOR ALBERT - Nor know you
Who slew him?

COUNT SIEGENDORF - I could only guess at one,
And he to me a stranger, unconnected,
As unemployed. Except by one day's knowledge,
I never saw the man who was suspected.

PRIOR ALBERT - Then you are free from guilt.

COUNT SIEGENDORF - (eagerly) Oh! am I?—say!

PRIOR ALBERT - You have said so, and know best.

COUNT SIEGENDORF - Father! I have spoken
The truth, and nought but truth, if not the whole;
Yet say I am not guilty! for the blood
Of this man weighs on me, as if I shed it,
Though, by the Power who abhorreth human blood,
I did not!—nay, once spared it, when I might
And could—aye, perhaps, should (if our self-safety
Be e'er excusable in such defences
Against the attacks of over-potent foes):
But pray for him, for me, and all my house;
For, as I said, though I be innocent,
I know not why, a like remorse is on me,
As if he had fallen by me or mine. Pray for me,
Father! I have prayed myself in vain.

PRIOR ALBERT - I will.
Be comforted! You are innocent, and should
Be calm as innocence.

COUNT SIEGENDORF - But calmness is not
Always the attribute of innocence.
I feel it is not.

PRIOR ALBERT - But it will be so,
When the mind gathers up its truth within it.
Remember the great festival to-morrow,
In which you rank amidst our chiefest nobles,
As well as your brave son; and smooth your aspect,
Nor in the general orison of thanks
For bloodshed stopt, let blood you shed not rise,
A cloud, upon your thoughts. This were to be
Too sensitive. Take comfort, and forget
Such things, and leave remorse unto the guilty.

[Exeunt.

ACT V

SCENE I. A Large and Magnificent Gothic Hall in the Castle of Siegendorf, Decorated with Trophies, Banners, and Arms of that Family.

Enter ARNHEIM and MEISTER, attendants of COUNT SIEGENDORF.

ARNHEIM - Be quick! the Count will soon return: the ladies
Already are at the portal. Have you sent
The messengers in search of him he seeks for?

MEISTER - I have, in all directions, over Prague,
As far as the man's dress and figure could
By your description track him. The devil take
These revels and processions! All the pleasure
(If such there be) must fall to the spectators,—
I'm sure none doth to us who make the show.

ARNHEIM - Go to! my Lady Countess comes.

MEISTER - I'd rather
Ride a day's hunting on an outworn jade,
Than follow in the train of a great man,
In these dull pageantries.

ARNHEIM - Begone! and rail
Within.

[Exeunt.

Enter the COUNTESS JOSEPHINE SIEGENDORF and IDA STRALENHEIM.

JOSEPHINE - Well, Heaven be praised! the show is over.

IDA STRALENHEIM - How can you say so? Never have I dreamt
Of aught so beautiful. The flowers, the boughs,
The banners, and the nobles, and the knights,
The gems, the robes, the plumes, the happy faces,
The coursers, and the incense, and the sun
Streaming through the stained windows, even the tombs,
Which looked so calm, and the celestial hymns,
Which seemed as if they rather came from Heaven
Than mounted there—the bursting organ's peal
Rolling on high like an harmonious thunder;
The white robes and the lifted eyes; the world
At peace! and all at peace with one another!
Oh, my sweet mother!

[Embracing JOSEPHINE.

JOSEPHINE - My belovéd child!
For such, I trust, thou shalt be shortly.

IDA STRALENHEIM - Oh!
I am so already. Feel how my heart beats!

JOSEPHINE - It does, my love; and never may it throb
With aught more bitter.

IDA STRALENHEIM - Never shall it do so!
How should it? What should make us grieve? I hate
To hear of sorrow: how can we be sad,
Who love each other so entirely? You,
The Count, and Ulric, and your daughter Ida.

JOSEPHINE - Poor child!

IDA STRALENHEIM - Do you pity me?

JOSEPHINE - No: I but envy,
And that in sorrow, not in the world's sense
Of the universal vice, if one vice be
More general than another.

IDA STRALENHEIM - I'll not hear
A word against a world which still contains
You and my Ulric. Did you ever see
Aught like him? How he towered amongst them all!
How all eyes followed him! The flowers fell faster—
Rained from each lattice at his feet, methought,
Than before all the rest; and where he trod
I dare be sworn that they grow still, nor e'er
Will wither.

JOSEPHINE - You will spoil him, little flatterer,
If he should hear you.

IDA STRALENHEIM - But he never will.
I dare not say so much to him—I fear him.

JOSEPHINE - Why so? he loves you well.

IDA STRALENHEIM - But I can never
Shape my thoughts of him into words to him:
Besides, he sometimes frightens me.

JOSEPHINE - How so?
IDA STRALENHEIM - A cloud comes o'er his blue eyes suddenly,
Yet he says nothing.

JOSEPHINE - It is nothing: all men,
Especially in these dark troublous times,
Have much to think of.

IDA STRALENHEIM - But I cannot think
Of aught save him.

JOSEPHINE - Yet there are other men,
In the world's eye, as goodly. There's, for instance,
The young Count Waldorf, who scarce once withdrew
His eyes from yours to-day.

IDA STRALENHEIM - I did not see him,
But Ulric. Did you not see at the moment
When all knelt, and I wept? and yet, methought,
Through my fast tears, though they were thick and warm,
I saw him smiling on me.

JOSEPHINE - I could not
See aught save Heaven, to which my eyes were raised,
Together with the people's.

IDA STRALENHEIM - I thought too
Of Heaven, although I looked on Ulric.

JOSEPHINE - Come,
Let us retire! they will be here anon,
Expectant of the banquet. We will lay
Aside these nodding plumes and dragging trains.

IDA STRALENHEIM - And, above all, these stiff and heavy jewels,
Which make my head and heart ache, as both throb
Beneath their glitter o'er my brow and zone.
Dear mother, I am with you.

Enter COUNT SIEGENDORF, in full dress, from the solemnity, and LUDWIG.

COUNT SIEGENDORF - Is he not found?

LUDWIG - Strict search is making every where; and if
The man be in Prague, be sure he will be found.

COUNT SIEGENDORF - Where's Ulric?

LUDWIG - He rode round the other way
With some young nobles; but he left them soon;
And, if I err not, not a minute since
I heard his Excellency, with his train,
Gallop o'er the west drawbridge.

Enter ULRIC, splendidly dressed.

COUNT SIEGENDORF - (to LUDWIG) See they cease not
Their quest of him I have described.

[Exit LUDWIG.

Oh, Ulric!
How have I longed for thee!

ULRIC - Your wish is granted—
Behold me!

COUNT SIEGENDORF - I have seen the murderer.

ULRIC - Whom? Where?

COUNT SIEGENDORF - The Hungarian, who slew Stralenheim.

ULRIC - You dream.

COUNT SIEGENDORF - I live! and as I live, I saw him—
Heard him! he dared to utter even my name.

ULRIC - What name?

COUNT SIEGENDORF - Werner! 'twas mine.

ULRIC - It must be so
No more: forget it.

COUNT SIEGENDORF - Never! never! all
My destinies were woven in that name:
It will not be engraved upon my tomb,
But it may lead me there.

ULRIC - To the point—the Hungarian?

COUNT SIEGENDORF - Listen!—The church was thronged: the hymn was raised;
"Te Deum" pealed from nations rather than
From choirs, in one great cry of "God be praised"
For one day's peace, after thrice ten dread years,
Each bloodier than the former: I arose,
With all the nobles, and as I looked down
Along the lines of lifted faces,—from
Our bannered and escutcheoned gallery, I
Saw, like a flash of lightning (for I saw
A moment and no more), what struck me sightless
To all else—the Hungarian's face! I grew
Sick; and when I recovered from the mist
Which curled about my senses, and again
Looked down, I saw him not. The thanksgiving

Was over, and we marched back in procession.

ULRIC - Continue.

COUNT SIEGENDORF - When we reached the Muldau's bridge,
The joyous crowd above, the numberless
Barks manned with revellers in their best garbs,
Which shot along the glancing tide below,
The decorated street, the long array,
The clashing music, and the thundering
Of far artillery, which seemed to bid
A long and loud farewell to its great doings,
The standards o'er me, and the tramplings round,
The roar of rushing thousands,—all—all could not
Chase this man from my mind, although my senses
No longer held him palpable.

ULRIC - You saw him
No more, then?

COUNT SIEGENDORF - I looked, as a dying soldier
Looks at a draught of water, for this man;
But still I saw him not; but in his stead—

ULRIC - What in his stead?

COUNT SIEGENDORF - My eye for ever fell
Upon your dancing crest; the loftiest.
As on the loftiest and the loveliest head,
It rose the highest of the stream of plumes,
Which overflowed the glittering streets of Prague.

ULRIC - What's this to the Hungarian?

COUNT SIEGENDORF - Much! for I
Had almost then forgot him in my son;
When just as the artillery ceased, and paused
The music, and the crowd embraced in lieu
Of shouting, I heard in a deep, low voice,
Distinct and keener far upon my ear
Than the late cannon's volume, this word—"Werner!"

ULRIC - Uttered by—

COUNT SIEGENDORF - HIM! I turned—and saw—and fell.

ULRIC - And wherefore? Were you seen?

COUNT SIEGENDORF - The officious care
Of those around me dragged me from the spot,
Seeing my faintness, ignorant of the cause:

You, too, were too remote in the procession
(The old nobles being divided from their children)
To aid me.

ULRIC - But I'll aid you now.

COUNT SIEGENDORF - In what?

ULRIC - In searching for this man, or—When he's found,
What shall we do with him?

COUNT SIEGENDORF - I know not that.

ULRIC - Then wherefore seek?

COUNT SIEGENDORF - Because I cannot rest
Till he is found. His fate, and Stralenheim's,
And ours, seem intertwisted! nor can be
Unravelled, till—

Enter an ATTENDANT.

ATTENDANT - A stranger to wait on
Your Excellency.

COUNT SIEGENDORF - Who?

ATTENDANT He gave no name.

COUNT SIEGENDORF - Admit him, ne'ertheless.

[The ATTENDANT introduces GABOR, and afterwards exit.

Ah!

GABOR - 'Tis then Werner!

COUNT SIEGENDORF - (haughtily).
The same you knew, sir, by that name; and you!

GABOR - (looking round).
I recognise you both: father and son,
It seems. Count, I have heard that you, or yours,
Have lately been in search of me: I am here.

COUNT SIEGENDORF - I have sought you, and have found you: you are charged
(Your own heart may inform you why) with such
A crime as—

[He pauses.

GABOR - Give it utterance, and then
I'll meet the consequences.

COUNT SIEGENDORF - You shall do so—
Unless—

GABOR - First, who accuses me?

COUNT SIEGENDORF - All things,
If not all men: the universal rumour—
My own presence on the spot—the place—the time—
And every speck of circumstance unite
To fix the blot on you.

GABOR - And on me only?
Pause ere you answer: is no other name,
Save mine, stained in this business?

COUNT SIEGENDORF - Trifling villain!
Who play'st with thine own guilt! Of all that breathe
Thou best dost know the innocence of him
'Gainst whom thy breath would blow thy bloody slander.
But I will talk no further with a wretch,
Further than justice asks. Answer at once,
And without quibbling, to my charge.

GABOR - 'Tis false!

COUNT SIEGENDORF - Who says so?

GABOR - I.

COUNT SIEGENDORF - And how disprove it?

GABOR - By
The presence of the murderer.

COUNT SIEGENDORF - Name him.

GABOR - He
May have more names than one. Your Lordship had so
Once on a time.

COUNT SIEGENDORF - If you mean me, I dare
Your utmost.

GABOR - You may do so, and in safety;
I know the assassin.

COUNT SIEGENDORF - Where is he?

GABOR - (pointing to ULRIC) Beside you!

[ULRIC rushes forward to attack GABOR; SIEGENDORF interposes.

COUNT SIEGENDORF - Liar and fiend! but you shall not be slain;
These walls are mine, and you are safe within them.
Ulric, repel this calumny, as I

[He turns to ULRIC.

Will do. I avow it is a growth so monstrous,
I could not deem it earth-born: but be calm;
It will refute itself. But touch him not.

[ULRIC endeavours to compose himself.

GABOR - Look at him, Count, and then hear me.

COUNT SIEGENDORF - (first to GABOR, and then looking at ULRIC).
I hear thee.
My God! you look—

ULRIC - How?

COUNT SIEGENDORF - As on that dread night,
When we met in the garden.

ULRIC - (composing himself). It is nothing.

GABOR - Count, you are bound to hear me. I came hither
Not seeking you, but sought. When I knelt down
Amidst the people in the church, I dreamed not
To find the beggared Werner in the seat
Of Senators and Princes; but you have called me,
And we have met.

COUNT SIEGENDORF - Go on, sir.

GABOR - Ere I do so,
Allow me to inquire, who profited
By Stralenheim's death? Was't I—as poor as ever;
And poorer by suspicion on my name!
The Baron lost in that last outrage neither
Jewels nor gold; his life alone was sought.—
A life which stood between the claims of others
To honours and estates scarce less than princely.

COUNT SIEGENDORF - These hints, as vague as vain, attach no less
To me than to my son.

GABOR - I can't help that.

But let the consequence alight on him
Who feels himself the guilty one amongst us.
I speak to you, Count Siegendorf, because
I know you innocent, and deem you just.
But ere I can proceed—dare you protect me?
Dare you command me?

[SIEGENDORF first looks at the Hungarian, and then at ULRIC, who has unbuckled his sabre, and is drawing lines with it on the floor—still in its sheath.

ULRIC - (looks at his father, and says,) Let the man go on!

GABOR - I am unarmed, Count, bid your son lay down
His sabre.

ULRIC - (offers it to him contemptuously). Take it.

GABOR - No, sir, 'tis enough
That we are both unarmed—I would not choose
To wear a steel which may be stained with more
Blood than came there in battle.

ULRIC - (casts the sabre from him in contempt). It—or some
Such other weapon in my hand—spared yours
Once, when disarmed and at my mercy.

GABOR - True—
I have not forgotten it: you spared me for
Your own especial purpose—to sustain
An ignominy not my own.

ULRIC - Proceed.
The tale is doubtless worthy the relater.
But is it of my father to hear further? [To SIEGENDORF.

COUNT SIEGENDORF - (takes his son by the hand).
My son, I know my own innocence, and doubt not
Of yours—but I have promised this man patience;
Let him continue.

GABOR - I will not detain you,
By speaking of myself much: I began
Life early—and am what the world has made me.
At Frankfort on the Oder, where I passed
A winter in obscurity, it was
My chance at several places of resort
(Which I frequented sometimes, but not often)
To hear related a strange circumstance
In February last. A martial force,
Sent by the state, had, after strong resistance,
Secured a band of desperate men, supposed

Marauders from the hostile camp.—They proved,
However, not to be so—but banditti,
Whom either accident or enterprise
Had carried from their usual haunt—the forests
Which skirt Bohemia—even into Lusatia.
Many amongst them were reported of
High rank—and martial law slept for a time.
At last they were escorted o'er the frontiers,
And placed beneath the civil jurisdiction
Of the free town of Frankfort. Of their fate
I know no more.

COUNT SIEGENDORF - And what is this to Ulric?

GABOR - Amongst them there was said to be one man
Of wonderful endowments:—birth and fortune,
Youth, strength, and beauty, almost superhuman,
And courage as unrivalled, were proclaimed
His by the public rumour; and his sway,
Not only over his associates, but
His judges, was attributed to witchcraft,
Such was his influence:—I have no great faith
In any magic save that of the mine—
I therefore deemed him wealthy.—But my soul
Was roused with various feelings to seek out
This prodigy, if only to behold him.

COUNT SIEGENDORF - And did you so?

GABOR - You'll hear. Chance favoured me:
A popular affray in the public square
Drew crowds together—it was one of those
Occasions where men's souls look out of them,
And show them as they are—even in their faces:
The moment my eye met his, I exclaimed,
"This is the man!" though he was then, as since,
With the nobles of the city. I felt sure
I had not erred, and watched him long and nearly;
I noted down his form—his gesture—features,
Stature, and bearing—and amidst them all,
'Midst every natural and acquired distinction,
I could discern, methought, the assassin's eye
And gladiator's heart.

ULRIC - (smiling) The tale sounds well.

GABOR - And may sound better.—He appeared to me
One of those beings to whom Fortune bends,
As she doth to the daring—and on whom
The fates of others oft depend; besides,
An indescribable sensation drew me

Near to this man, as if my point of fortune
Was to be fixed by him.—There I was wrong.

COUNT SIEGENDORF - And may not be right now.

GABOR - I followed him,
Solicited his notice—and obtained it—
Though not his friendship:—it was his intention
To leave the city privately—we left it
Together—and together we arrived
In the poor town where Werner was concealed,
And Stralenheim was succoured—Now we are on
The verge—dare you hear further?

COUNT SIEGENDORF - I must do so—
Or I have heard too much.

GABOR - I saw in you
A man above his station—and if not
So high, as now I find you, in my then
Conceptions, 'twas that I had rarely seen
Men such as you appeared in height of mind,
In the most high of worldly rank; you were
Poor, even to all save rags: I would have shared
My purse, though slender, with you—you refused it.

COUNT SIEGENDORF - Doth my refusal make a debt to you,
That thus you urge it?

GABOR - Still you owe me something,
Though not for that; and I owed you my safety,
At least my seeming safety, when the slaves
Of Stralenheim pursued me on the grounds
That I had robbed him.

COUNT SIEGENDORF - I concealed you—I,
Whom and whose house you arraign, reviving viper!

GABOR - I accuse no man—save in my defence.
You, Count, have made yourself accuser—judge:
Your hall's my court, your heart is my tribunal.
Be just, and I'll be merciful!

COUNT SIEGENDORF - You merciful?—
You! Base calumniator!

GABOR - I. 'Twill rest
With me at last to be so. You concealed me—
In secret passages known to yourself,
You said, and to none else. At dead of night,
Weary with watching in the dark, and dubious

Of tracing back my way, I saw a glimmer,
Through distant crannies, of a twinkling light:
I followed it, and reached a door—a secret
Portal—which opened to the chamber, where,
With cautious hand and slow, having first undone
As much as made a crevice of the fastening,
I looked through and beheld a purple bed,
And on it Stralenheim!—

COUNT SIEGENDORF - Asleep! And yet
You slew him!—Wretch!

GABOR - He was already slain,
And bleeding like a sacrifice. My own
Blood became ice.

COUNT SIEGENDORF - But he was all alone!
You saw none else? You did not see the—

[He pauses from agitation.

GABOR - No,
He, whom you dare not name, nor even I
Scarce dare to recollect, was not then in
The chamber.

COUNT SIEGENDORF - (to ULRIC). Then, my boy! thou art guiltless still—
Thou bad'st me say I was so once.—Oh! now
Do thou as much.

GABOR - Be patient! I can not
Recede now, though it shake the very walls
Which frown above us. You remember,—or
If not, your son does,—that the locks were changed
Beneath his chief inspection on the morn
Which led to this same night: how he had entered
He best knows—but within an antechamber,
The door of which was half ajar, I saw
A man who washed his bloody hands, and oft
With stern and anxious glance gazed back upon—
The bleeding body—but it moved no more.

COUNT SIEGENDORF - Oh! God of fathers!

GABOR - I beheld his features
As I see yours—but yours they were not, though
Resembling them—behold them in Count Ulric's!
Distinct as I beheld them, though the expression
Is not now what it then was!—but it was so
When I first charged him with the crime—so lately.

COUNT SIEGENDORF - This is so—

GABOR - (interrupting him) Nay—but hear me to the end!
Now you must do so.—I conceived myself
Betrayed by you and him (for now I saw
There was some tie between you) into this
Pretended den of refuge, to become
The victim of your guilt; and my first thought
Was vengeance: but though armed with a short poniard
(Having left my sword without), I was no match
For him at any time, as had been proved
That morning—either in address or force.
I turned and fled—i' the dark: chance rather than
Skill made me gain the secret door of the hall,
And thence the chamber where you slept: if I
Had found you waking, Heaven alone can tell
What vengeance and suspicion might have prompted;
But ne'er slept guilt as Werner slept that night.

COUNT SIEGENDORF - And yet I had horrid dreams! and such brief sleep,
The stars had not gone down when I awoke.
Why didst thou spare me? I dreamt of my father—
And now my dream is out!

GABOR - 'Tis not my fault,
If I have read it.—Well! I fled and hid me—
Chance led me here after so many moons—
And showed me Werner in Count Siegendorf!
Werner, whom I had sought in huts in vain,
Inhabited the palace of a sovereign!
You sought me and have found me—now you know
My secret, and may weigh its worth.

COUNT SIEGENDORF - (after a pause) Indeed!

GABOR - Is it revenge or justice which inspires
Your meditation?

COUNT SIEGENDORF - Neither—I was weighing
The value of your secret.

GABOR - You shall know it
At once:—When you were poor, and I, though poor,
Rich enough to relieve such poverty
As might have envied mine, I offered you
My purse—you would not share it:—I'll be franker
With you: you are wealthy, noble, trusted by
The imperial powers—you understand me?

COUNT SIEGENDORF - Yes.

GABOR - Not quite. You think me venal, and scarce true:
'Tis no less true, however, that my fortunes
Have made me both at present. You shall aid me:
I would have aided you—and also have
Been somewhat damaged in my name to save
Yours and your son's. Weigh well what I have said.

COUNT SIEGENDORF - Dare you await the event of a few minutes'
Deliberation?

GABOR - (casts his eyes on ULRIC, who is leaning against a pillar).
If I should do so?

COUNT SIEGENDORF - I pledge my life for yours. Withdraw into
This tower.

[Opens a turret-door.

GABOR - (hesitatingly). This is the second safe asylum
You have offered me.

COUNT SIEGENDORF - And was not the first so?

GABOR - I know not that even now—but will approve
The second. I have still a further shield.—
I did not enter Prague alone; and should I
Be put to rest with Stralenheim, there are
Some tongues without will wag in my behalf.
Be brief in your decision!

COUNT SIEGENDORF - I will be so.—
My word is sacred and irrevocable
Within these walls, but it extends no further.

GABOR - I'll take it for so much.

COUNT SIEGENDORF - (points to ULRIC'S sabre, still upon the ground).
Take also that—
I saw you eye it eagerly, and him
Distrustfully.

GABOR - (takes up the sabre). I will; and so provide
To sell my life—not cheaply.

[GABOR goes into the turret, which SIEGENDORF closes.

COUNT SIEGENDORF - (advances to ULRIC). Now, Count Ulric!
For son I dare not call thee—What say'st thou?

ULRIC - His tale is true.

COUNT SIEGENDORF - True, monster!

ULRIC - Most true, father!
And you did well to listen to it: what
We know, we can provide against. He must
Be silenced.

COUNT SIEGENDORF - Aye, with half of my domains;
And with the other half, could he and thou
Unsay this villany.

ULRIC - It is no time
For trifling or dissembling. I have said
His story's true; and he too must be silenced.

COUNT SIEGENDORF - How so?

ULRIC - As Stralenheim is. Are you so dull
As never to have hit on this before?
When we met in the garden, what except
Discovery in the act could make me know
His death? Or had the Prince's household been
Then summoned, would the cry for the police
Been left to such a stranger? Or should I
Have loitered on the way? Or could you, Werner,
The object of the Baron's hate and fears,
Have fled, unless by many an hour before
Suspicion woke? I sought and fathomed you,
Doubting if you were false or feeble: I
Perceived you were the latter: and yet so
Confiding have I found you, that I doubted
At times your weakness.

COUNT SIEGENDORF - Parricide! no less
Than common stabber! What deed of my life,
Or thought of mine, could make you deem me fit
For your accomplice?

ULRIC - Father, do not raise
The devil you cannot lay between us. This
Is time for union and for action, not
For family disputes. While you were tortured,
Could I be calm? Think you that I have heard
This fellow's tale without some feeling?—You
Have taught me feeling for you and myself;
For whom or what else did you ever teach it?

COUNT SIEGENDORF - Oh! my dead father's curse! 'tis working now.

ULRIC - Let it work on! the grave will keep it down!
Ashes are feeble foes: it is more easy

To baffle such, than countermine a mole,
Which winds its blind but living path beneath you.
Yet hear me still!—If you condemn me, yet,
Remember who hath taught me once too often
To listen to him! Who proclaimed to me
That there were crimes made venial by the occasion?
That passion was our nature? that the goods
Of Heaven waited on the goods of fortune?
Who showed me his humanity secured
By his nerves only? Who deprived me of
All power to vindicate myself and race
In open day? By his disgrace which stamped
(It might be) bastardy on me, and on
Himself—a felon's brand! The man who is
At once both warm and weak invites to deeds
He longs to do, but dare not. Is it strange
That I should act what you could think? We have done
With right and wrong; and now must only ponder
Upon effects, not causes. Stralenheim,
Whose life I saved from impulse, as unknown,
I would have saved a peasant's or a dog's, I slew
Known as our foe—but not from vengeance. He
Was a rock in our way which I cut through,
As doth the bolt, because it stood between us
And our true destination—but not idly.
As stranger I preserved him, and he owed me
His life: when due, I but resumed the debt.
He, you, and I stood o'er a gulf wherein
I have plunged our enemy. You kindled first
The torch—you showed the path; now trace me that
Of safety—or let me!

COUNT SIEGENDORF - I have done with life!

ULRIC - Let us have done with that which cankers life—
Familiar feuds and vain recriminations
Of things which cannot be undone. We have
No more to learn or hide: I know no fear,
And have within these very walls men who
(Although you know them not) dare venture all things.
You stand high with the state; what passes here
Will not excite her too great curiosity:
Keep your own secret, keep a steady eye,
Stir not, and speak not;—leave the rest to me:
We must have no third babblers thrust between us.

[Exit ULRIC.

COUNT SIEGENDORF - (solus). Am I awake? are these my father's halls?
And you—my son? My son! mine! I who have ever
Abhorred both mystery and blood, and yet

Am plunged into the deepest hell of both!
I must be speedy, or more will be shed—
The Hungarian's!—Ulric—he hath partisans,
It seems: I might have guessed as much. Oh fool!
Wolves prowl in company. He hath the key
(As I too) of the opposite door which leads
Into the turret. Now then! or once more
To be the father of fresh crimes, no less
Than of the criminal! Ho! Gabor! Gabor!

[Exit into the turret, closing the door after him.

SCENE II. The Interior of the Turret.

GABOR and SIEGENDORF.

GABOR - Who calls?

COUNT SIEGENDORF - I—Siegendorf! Take these and fly!
Lose not a moment!

[Tears off a diamond star and other jewels, and thrusts them into GABOR'S hand.

GABOR - What am I to do
With these?

COUNT SIEGENDORF - Whate'er you will: sell them, or hoard,
And prosper; but delay not, or you are lost!

GABOR - You pledged your honour for my safety!

COUNT SIEGENDORF - And
Must thus redeem it. Fly! I am not master,
It seems, of my own castle—of my own
Retainers—nay, even of these very walls,
Or I would bid them fall and crush me! Fly!
Or you will be slain by—

GABOR - Is it even so?
Farewell, then! Recollect, however, Count,
You sought this fatal interview!

COUNT SIEGENDORF - I did:
Let it not be more fatal still!—Begone!

GABOR - By the same path I entered?

COUNT SIEGENDORF - Yes; that's safe still;
But loiter not in Prague;—you do not know

With whom you have to deal.

GABOR - I know too well—
And knew it ere yourself, unhappy Sire!
Farewell!

[Exit GABOR.

COUNT SIEGENDORF - (solus and listening).
He hath cleared the staircase. Ah! I hear
The door sound loud behind him! He is safe!
Safe!—Oh, my father's spirit!—I am faint—

[He leans down upon a stone seat, near the wall of the tower, in a drooping posture.

Enter ULRIC with others armed, and with weapons drawn.

ULRIC - Despatch!—he's there!

LUDWIG - The Count, my Lord!

ULRIC - (recognizing SIEGENDORF) You here, sir!

COUNT SIEGENDORF - Yes: if you want another victim, strike!

ULRIC - (seeing him stript of his jewels).
Where is the ruffian who hath plundered you?
Vassals, despatch in search of him! You see
'Twas as I said—the wretch hath stript my father
Of jewels which might form a Prince's heir-loom!
Away! I'll follow you forthwith.

[Exeunt all but SIEGENDORF and ULRIC.

What's this?
Where is the villain?

COUNT SIEGENDORF - There are two, sir: which
Are you in quest of?

ULRIC - Let us hear no more
Of this: he must be found. You have not let him
Escape?

COUNT SIEGENDORF - He's gone.

ULRIC - With your connivance?

COUNT SIEGENDORF - With
My fullest, freest aid.

ULRIC - Then fare you well!

[ULRIC is going.

COUNT SIEGENDORF - Stop! I command—entreat—implore! Oh, Ulric!
Will you then leave me?

ULRIC - What! remain to be
Denounced—dragged, it may be, in chains; and all
By your inherent weakness, half-humanity,
Selfish remorse, and temporizing pity,
That sacrifices your whole race to save
A wretch to profit by our ruin! No, Count,
Henceforth you have no son!

COUNT SIEGENDORF - I never had one;
And would you ne'er had borne the useless name!
Where will you go? I would not send you forth
Without protection.

ULRIC - Leave that unto me.
I am not alone; nor merely the vain heir
Of your domains; a thousand, aye, ten thousand
Swords, hearts, and hands are mine.

COUNT SIEGENDORF - The foresters!
With whom the Hungarian found you first at Frankfort!

ULRIC - Yes—men—who are worthy of the name! Go tell
Your Senators that they look well to Prague;
Their Feast of Peace was early for the times;
There are more spirits abroad than have been laid
With Wallenstein!

Enter JOSEPHINE and IDA.

JOSEPHINE - What is't we hear? My Siegendorf!
Thank Heaven, I see you safe!

COUNT SIEGENDORF - Safe!

IDA STRALENHEIM - Yes, dear father!

COUNT SIEGENDORF - No, no; I have no children: never more
Call me by that worst name of parent.

JOSEPHINE - What
Means my good Lord?

COUNT SIEGENDORF - That you have given birth
To a demon!

IDA STRALENHEIM - (taking ULRIC'S hand). Who shall dare say this of Ulric?

COUNT SIEGENDORF - Ida, beware! there's blood upon that hand.

IDA STRALENHEIM - (stooping to kiss it).
I'd kiss it off, though it were mine.

COUNT SIEGENDORF - It is so!

ULRIC - Away! it is your father's!

[Exit ULRIC.

IDA STRALENHEIM - Oh, great God!
And I have loved this man!

[IDA falls senseless—JOSEPHINE stands speechless with horror.

COUNT SIEGENDORF - The wretch hath slain
Them both!—My Josephine! we are now alone!
Would we had ever been so!—All is over
For me!—Now open wide, my sire, thy grave;
Thy curse hath dug it deeper for thy son
In mine!—The race of Siegendorf is past.

The end of the fifth act and the Drama.

NOTE TO THE INTRODUCTION TO WERNER

In an article entitled, "Did Byron write Werner?" which appeared in the Nineteenth Century (August, 1899, vol. 46, pp. 243-250), the Hon. F. Leveson Gower undertakes to prove that Werner was not written by Lord Byron, but by Georgiana, Duchess of Devonshire (born June 9, 1757, died March 30, 1806). He adduces, in support of this claim, (1) a statement made to him by his sister, the late Lady Georgiana Fullerton, to the effect that their grandmother, the duchess, "wrote the poem and gave the MS. to her niece, Lady Caroline Ponsonby (better known as Lady Caroline Lamb), and that she, some years later, handed it over to Lord Byron, who, in 1822, published it in his own name;" (2) a letter written in 1822 by his mother, Lady Granville, to her sister, Lady Carlisle, which asserts that their mother, the duchess, "wrote an entire tragedy from Miss Lee's Kreutzner the Hungarian (sic)," and that the MS. had been sent to her by Lady Caroline's brother, Mr. William Ponsonby, and was in her possession; (3) another letter of Lady Granville's, dated December 3, 1822, in which she informs her sister that her husband, Lord Granville, had promised to read Werner aloud to her (i.e. Byron's Werner, published November 23, 1822), a promise which, if fulfilled, must have revealed one of two things—the existence of two dramas based on Miss Lee's Kruitzner, or the identity of Byron's version with that of the duchess. Now, argues Mr. Leveson Gower, if Lady Granville had known that two dramas were in existence, she would not have allowed her daughter, Lady Georgiana Fullerton, to believe "that the duchess was the author of the published poem."

I will deal with the external evidence first. Practically it amounts to this: (1) that Lady Granville knew that her mother, the Duchess of Devonshire, dramatized Miss Lee's Kruitzner; and (2) that Lady Georgiana Fullerton believed that the duchess gave the MS. of her play to Lady Caroline Ponsonby, and that, many years after, Lady Caroline handed it over to Byron.

The external evidence establishes the fact that the Duchess of Devonshire dramatized Kruitzner, but it does not prove that Byron purloined her adaptation. It records an unverified impression on the part of the duchess's granddaughter, that the MS. of a play written between the years 1801-1806, passed into Byron's hands about the year 1813; that he took a copy of the MS.; and that in 1821-22 he caused his copy to be retranscribed and published under his own name.

But Mr. Leveson Gower appeals to internal as well as external evidence, (1) He regards the great inferiority of Werner to Byron's published plays, and to the genuine (hitherto) unpublished first act, together with the wholesale plagiarisms from Miss Lee's story, as an additional proof that the work was none of his. (2) He notes, as a suspicious circumstance, that "while the rough copies of his other poems have been preserved, no rough copy of Werner is to be found."

In conclusion, he deals with two possible objections which may be brought against his theory: (1) that Byron would not have incurred the risk of detection at the hands of the owners of the duchess's MS.; and (2) that a great poet of assured fame and reputation could have had no possible motive for perpetrating a literary fraud. The first objection he answers by assuming that Byron would have counted on the reluctance of the "Ponsonby family and the daughters of the Duchess" to rake up the ashes of old scandals; the second, by pointing out that, in 1822, he was making "frantic endeavours to obtain money, not for himself, but to help the cause of Greece."

(1) With regard to the marked inferiority of Werner to Byron's other plays, and the relative proportion of adapted to original matter, Mr. Leveson Gower appears to have been misled by the disingenuous criticism of Maginn and other contemporary reviewers (vide the Introduction, etc., p. 326). There is no such inferiority, and the plagiarisms, which were duly acknowledged, are confined to certain limited portions of the play. (2) There is nothing unusual in the fact that the rough draft of Werner cannot be found. In fact, but few of the early drafts of the dramas and other poems written in the later Italian days ever reached Murray's hands, or are still in existence. The fair copy for the printer alone was sent home. The time had gone by when Byron's publisher, who was also his friend, would stipulate that "all the original MSS., copies and scraps" should fall to his share. But no argument can be founded on so insignificant a circumstance.

Finally, the argument on which Mr. Leveson Gower dwells at some length, that Byron's "motive" for perpetrating a literary fraud was the necessity for raising money for the cause of Greek independence, is refuted by the fact that Werner was begun in December, 1821, and finished in January, 1822, and that it was not till the spring of 1823 that he was elected a member of the Greek Committee, or had any occasion to raise funds for the maintenance of troops or the general expenses of the war. So far from attempting to raise money by Werner, in letters to Murray, dated March 6, October 24, November 18, 1822, he emphatically waives the question of "terms," and makes no demand or request for money whatever. It was not till December 23, 1823 (Letters, 1901, vi. 287), two years after the play had been written, that he speaks of applying the two or three hundred pounds which the copyright of Werner might be worth, to the maintenance of armed men in the service of the Provisional Government. He could not have "purloined" and palmed off as his own the duchess's version of Miss Lee's story in order to raise money for a purpose which had not arisen. He had no intention at first or last of presenting the copyright of Werner to Murray or Hunt, but he was willing to wait for his money, and had no motive for raising funds by an illegal and dishonourable trick.

That Byron did not write Werner is, surely, non-proven on the external and internal evidence adduced by Mr. Leveson Gower. On the other hand, there is abundant evidence, both external and internal, that, apart from his acknowledged indebtedness to Miss Lee's story, he did write Werner.

To take the external evidence first. On the first page of Mrs. Shelley's transcript of Werner, Byron inserted the date, "Dec. 18, 1821," and on the last he wrote "[The End] of fifth act of the Drama. B. Pisa. Jy 21. 1822."

Turning to the journal of Edward Williams (Shelley's Prose Works, 1880, iv. 318), I find the following entries:—

"December 21, 1821. Lord B. told me that he had commenced a tragedy from Miss Lee's German Tale ('Werner'), and had been fagging at it all day."

"January 8, 1822. Mary read us the first two acts of Lord B.'s Werner."

Again, in an unpublished diary of the same period it is recorded that Mrs. Shelley was engaged in the task of copying on January 17, 1822, and the eight following days, and that on January 25 she finished her transcript.

Again, Medwin (Conversations, 1824, p. 409) records the fact that Byron told him "that he had almost finished another play ... called Werner;" and (p. 412) "that Werner was written in twenty-eight days, and one entire act at a sitting." It is almost incredible that Byron should have recopied a copy of the duchess's play in order to impose on Mrs. Shelley and Williams and Medwin; and it is quite incredible that they were in the plot, and lent themselves to the deception. It is certain that both Williams and Medwin believed that Byron was the author of Werner, and it is certain that nothing would have induced Mrs. Shelley to be particeps criminis—to copy a play which was not Byron's, to be published as Byron's, and to suffer her copy to be fraudulently endorsed by her guilty accomplice.

The internal evidence of the genuineness of Werner is still more convincing. In the first place, there are numerous "undesigned coincidences," allusions, and phrases to be found in Werner and elsewhere in Byron's Poetical Works, which bear his sign-manual, and cannot be attributed to another writer; and, secondly, scattered through the play there are numerous lines, passages, allusions—"a cloud of witnesses" to their Byronic inspiration and creation.

Take the following parallels:—

Werner, act i. sc. 1, lines 693, 694—

"... as parchment on a drum,
Like Ziska's skin."

Age of Bronze, lines 133, 134—

"The time may come,
His name shall beat the alarm like Ziska's drum."

Werner, act ii. sc. 2, lines 177, 178—

"... save your throat
From the Raven-stone."

Manfred, act iii. (original version)—

"The raven sits
On the Raven-stone."

Werner, act ii. sc. 2, line 279—

"Things which had made this silkworm cast his skin."

Marino Faliero, act ii. sc. 2, line 115—

"... these swoln silkworms masters."

("Silkworm," as a term of contempt, is an Italianism.)

Werner, act iii. sc. 1, lines 288, 289—

"I fear that men must draw their chariots, as
They say kings did Sesostris'."

Age of Bronze, line 45—

"The new Sesostris, whose unharnessed kings."

Werner, act iii. sc. 3, lines 10, 11—

"... while the knoll
Of long-lived parents."

Childe Harold, Canto III. stanza xcvi. lines 5, 6—

"... is the knoll
Of what in me is sleepless."

(Byron is the authority for the use of "knoll" as a substantive.)

Or, compare the statement (see act i. sc. 1, line 213, sq.) that "A great personage ... is drowned below the ford, with five post-horses, A monkey and a mastiff—and a valet," with the corresponding passage in Kruitzner and in Byron's unfinished fragment; and note that "the monkey, the mastiff, and the valet," which formed part of Byron's retinue in 1821, are conspicuous by their absence from Miss Lee's story and the fragment.

Space precludes the quotation of further parallels, and for specimens of a score of passages which proclaim their author the following lines must suffice:—

Act i. sc. 1, lines 163-165—

"... although then

My passions were all living serpents, and
Twined like the Gorgon's round me."

Act iii. sc. 1, lines 264-268—

"... sound him with the gem;
'Twill sink into his venal soul like lead
Into the deep, and bring up slime and mud.
And ooze, too, from the bottom, as the lead doth
With its greased understratum."

Did Byron write Werner, or was it the Duchess of Devonshire?

(For a correspondence on the subject, see Literature, August 12, 19, 26, September 9, 1899.)

Lord Byron – A Short Biography

Byron, one of England's greatest poets, endured a quite difficult background. His father, Captain John "Mad Jack" Byron had married his second wife, the former Catherine Gordon, a descendant of Cardinal Beaton and heiress of the Gight estate in Aberdeenshire, Scotland for the same reason that he married his first: her money. Byron's mother-to-be had to sell her land and title to pay her new husband's debts and within two years the large estate of £23,500, had been squandered, leaving her with an annual income in trust of £150. In a move to avoid his creditors, Catherine accompanied her husband to France in 1786, but returned to England at the end of 1787 in order to give birth to her son on English soil.

George Gordon Byron was born on January 22nd 1788, in lodgings, at Holles Street in London although there is a conflicting account of him having been born in Dover.

He was christened, at St Marylebone Parish Church, George Gordon Byron, after his maternal grandfather, George Gordon of Gight, a descendant of James I of Scotland, who, in 1779, had committed suicide.

In 1790 Catherine moved back to Aberdeenshire and it was here that Byron spent his childhood. His father joined them in their lodgings in Queen Street, but the couple quickly separated. Catherine was prone to mood swings and melancholy. Her husband continued to borrow money from her and she fell deeper into debt. It was one of these "loans" that allowed him to travel to Valenciennes, France, where he died in 1791.

When Byron's great-uncle, the "wicked" Lord Byron, died on 21 May 1798, the 10-year-old boy became the 6th Baron Byron of Rochdale and inherited the ancestral home, Newstead Abbey, in Nottinghamshire. However the Abbey was in a state of disrepair and it was leased to Lord Grey de Ruthyn, and others for several years.

Catherine's parenting swung between either spoiling or indulging her son to stubbornly refusing every plea. Her drinking disgusted him, and he mocked her short and corpulent frame. She did retaliate and, in a fit of temper, once called him as "a lame brat", on account of his club-foot, an issue on which we was very sensitive. He referred to himself as "le diable boiteux" ("the limping devil").

Byron early education was taken at Aberdeen Grammar School, and in August 1799 he entered the school of Dr. William Glennie, in Dulwich. He was encouraged to exercise in moderation but could not restrain himself from "violent" bouts in an attempt to overcompensate for his deformed foot. His mother interfered, often withdrawing him from school, and resulting in him lacking discipline and neglecting his classical studies.

In 1801 he was sent to Harrow, where he remained until July 1805. Byron was an excellent orator but undistinguished student and an unskilled cricketer but strangely he did represent the school in the very first Eton v Harrow cricket match at Lord's in 1805.

Byron, always prone to over-indulge, fell in love with Mary Chaworth, whom he met while at school, and thence refused to return to Harrow in September 1803. His mother wrote, "He has no indisposition that I know of but love, desperate love, the worst of all maladies in my opinion. In short, the boy is distractedly in love with Miss Chaworth."

He did finally return in January 1804, and described his friends there; "My school friendships were with me passions for I was always violent." His nostalgic poems about his Harrow friendships, in his book Childish Recollections, published in 1806, talk of a "consciousness of sexual differences that may in the end make England untenable to him".

The following autumn he attended Trinity College, Cambridge, where he met and formed a close bond with John Edleston. On his "protégé" Byron wrote, "He has been my almost constant associate since October, 1805, when I entered Trinity College. His voice first attracted my attention, his countenance fixed it, and his manners attached me to him forever." In his memory Byron composed Thyrza, a series of elegies. In later years Byron described the affair as "a violent, though pure love and passion". The public were beginning to view homosexuality with increasing distaste and the law now specified such sanctions as public hanging against convicted or even suspected offenders. Though equally Byron may just be using 'pure' out of respect for Edleston's innocence, in contrast to the more sexually overt relations experienced at Harrow School. Byron is now thought of as bi-sexual though more fulfilled, on all levels, by women.

While not at school or college, Byron lived with his mother in Southwell, Nottinghamshire. While there, he cultivated friendships with Elizabeth Pigot and her brother, John, with whom he staged two plays for the entertainment of the local community. During this time, with the help of Elizabeth, who copied his rough drafts, he wrote his first volumes of poetry, Fugitive Pieces, which included poems written when Byron was only 14. However, it was promptly recalled and burned on the advice of his friend, the Reverend J. T. Becher, on account of its more amorous verses, particularly the poem To Mary.

Hours of Idleness, which collected many of the previous poems, along with recent compositions, was the culminating book. The savage, anonymous criticism this received in the Edinburgh Review prompted his first major satire, English Bards and Scotch Reviewers in 1809. This was put into the hands of his relative, R. C. Dallas, requesting him to "...get it published without his name". Although published anonymously Byron was generally known to be the author. The work so upset some of his critics they challenged Byron to a duel. Of course, over time, it became a mark of renown to be the target of Byron's pen.

Byron first took his seat in the House of Lords March 13th, 1809. He was a strong advocate of social reform, and one of the few Parliamentary defenders of the Luddites: specifically, he was against a death penalty for Luddite "frame breakers" in Nottinghamshire, who destroyed the textile machines that were putting them out of work. His first speech before the Lords, on February 27th, 1812, sarcastically referenced the "benefits" of automation, which he saw as producing inferior material as well as putting people out of work, and concluded the proposed law was only missing two things to be effective: "Twelve Butchers for a Jury and a Jeffries for a Judge!"

Two months later, Byron made another impassioned speech before the House in support of Catholic emancipation. He expressed opposition to the established religion because it was unfair to people who practiced other faiths.

Out of this period would follow several overtly political poems; Song for the Luddites (1816), The Landlords' Interest, Canto XIV of The Age of Bronze, Wellington: The Best of the Cut-Throats (1819) and The Intellectual Eunuch Castlereagh (1818).

Like his father Byron racked up numerous debts. His mother thought he had "reckless disregard for money" and lived in fear of her son's creditors.

Between 1809 to 1811, Byron went on the Grand Tour, then customary for a young nobleman. The Napoleonic Wars meant most of Europe had to be avoided, and he instead ventured south to the Mediterranean.

There is some correspondence among his circle of Cambridge friends that suggests that another motive was the hope of homosexual experience, and other theories saying that he was worried about a possible dalliance with a married woman, Mary Chaworth, his former love.

But other possibilities exist. Byron had read much about the Ottoman and Persian lands as a child, was attracted to Islam (especially Sufi mysticism), and later wrote, "With these countries, and events connected with them, all my really poetical feelings begin and end."

Byron began his trip in Portugal from where he wrote a letter to his friend Mr. Hodgson in which he describes his mastery of the Portuguese language, consisting mainly of swearing and insults. Byron particularly enjoyed his stay in Sintra that is described in Childe Harold's Pilgrimage as "glorious Eden". From Lisbon he travelled overland to Seville, Jerez de la Frontera, Cádiz, Gibraltar and from there by sea on to Malta and Greece.

While in Athens, Byron met 14-year-old Nicolò Giraud, who became quite close and taught him Italian. Byron sent Giraud to school at a monastery in Malta and in his will, though later taken out, bequeathed him a sizeable sum.

Byron then moved on to Smyrna, and then Constantinople on board HMS Salsette. While HMS Salsette was anchored awaiting Ottoman permission to dock at the city, on May 3rd, 1810 Byron and Lieutenant Ekenhead, of Salsette's Marines, swam the Hellespont. Byron commemorated this feat in the second canto of Don Juan.

When he sailed back to England in April 1811, he travelled, for a time, aboard the transport ship Hydra, which had on board the last large shipments of Lord Elgin's marbles, a piece of vandalism that Byron had longed railed against. The last leg of his voyage home was from Malta in aboard HMS Volage. He arrived at Sheerness, Kent, on July 14th. He was home after two years away.

On August 2nd, his mother died. "I had but one friend in the world," he exclaimed, "and she is gone."

The following year, 1812, Byron became a sensation with the publication, via his literary agent and family relative R. C. Dallas, of the first two cantos of 'Childe Harold's Pilgrimage'. He rapidly became the most brilliant star in the dazzling world of Regency London, sought after at every society venue, elected to several exclusive clubs, and frequented the most fashionable London drawing-rooms. His own words recall; "I awoke one morning and found myself famous". The Edinburgh Review allowed that Byron had "improved marvellously since his last appearance at our tribunal." He followed up his success with the poem's last two cantos, as well as four equally celebrated "Oriental Tales": The Giaour, The Bride of Abydos, The Corsair and Lara.

His affair with Lady Caroline Lamb (who called him "mad, bad and dangerous to know"), as well as other women and the constant pressure of debt, caused him to seek a suitable marriage i.e. marry wealth. One choice was Annabella Milbanke. But in 1813 he met again, after four years, his half-sister, Augusta Leigh. Rumours of incest constantly surrounded the pair; Augusta, who was married, gave birth on April 15th, 1814 to her third daughter, Elizabeth Medora Leigh, and Byron is suspected to be the father.

To escape from debts and rumours he now sought, in earnest, to marry Annabella, (said to be the likely heiress of a rich uncle). They married on January 2nd, 1815, and their daughter, Ada, was born in December of that year. However Byron's continuing obsession with Augusta and dalliances with others made their marriage a misery.

Annabella thought Byron insane and she left him, taking Ada, in January 1816 and began proceedings for a legal separation. For Byron the scandal of the separation, the continuing rumours about Augusta, and ever-increasing debts were to now force him to leave England.

He passed through Belgium and along the river Rhine and by the summer was settled at the Villa Diodati by Lake Geneva, Switzerland, with his personal physician, the young, brilliant, and handsome John William Polidori. There Byron befriended the poet Percy Bysshe Shelley, and his future wife Mary Godwin. He was also joined by Mary's stepsister, Claire Clairmont, with whom, almost inevitably, he had had an affair with in London.

Kept indoors at the Villa Diodati by the incessant rain during three days in June, the five turned to writing. Mary Shelley produced what would become Frankenstein, or The Modern Prometheus, and Polidori was inspired by a fragmentary story of Byron's, Fragment of a Novel, to produce The Vampyre, the progenitor of the romantic vampire genre.

Byron's story fragment was published as a postscript to Mazeppa; he also now wrote the third canto of Childe Harold.

Byron wintered in Venice, pausing his travels when he fell in love with Marianna Segati, in whose Venice house he was lodging, but who was soon replaced by 22-year-old Margarita Cogni; both women were married. Cogni, who could not read or write, left her husband to move into Byron's Venice house. Their fighting often caused Byron to spend nights in his gondola; when he asked her to leave the house, she threw herself into the Venetian canal.

In a visit to San Lazzaro degli Armeni in Venice, he began to immerse himself in Armenian culture. He learned the Armenian language, and attended many seminars about language and history. He co-authored English Grammar and Armenian in 1817, and Armenian Grammar and English in 1819, where he included quotations from classical and modern Armenian and later, in 1821, participated in the compilation of the English Armenian dictionary, and in the preface he mapped out the relationship of the Armenians with, and the oppression of, the Turkish "pashas" and the Persian satraps, and their struggle for liberation.

In 1817 after a visit to Rome and back in Venice, he wrote the fourth canto of Childe Harold and sold his ancestral home, Newstead Abbey, as well as publishing Manfred; A Dramatic Poem and , Cain; A Mystery.

Byron wrote the first five cantos of his renowned Don Juan between 1818 and 1820. And besides work and adventure there was always love. Women, of course, were always in evidence and the young Countess Teresa Guiccioli found her first love in Byron, who in turn asked her to elope with him. They lived in Ravenna between 1819 and 1821 where he continued Don Juan and also wrote the Ravenna Diary, My Dictionary and Recollections.

It was here that he now received visits from Percy Bysshe Shelley and Thomas Moore.

Of Byron's lifestyle in Ravenna Shelley informs us that; "Lord Byron gets up at two. I get up, quite contrary to my usual custom … at 12. After breakfast we sit talking till six. From six to eight we gallop through the pine forest which divide Ravenna from the sea; we then come home and dine, and sit up gossiping till six in the morning. I don't suppose this will kill me in a week or fortnight, but I shall not try it longer. Lord B.'s establishment consists, besides servants, of ten horses, eight enormous dogs, three monkeys, five cats, an eagle, a crow, and a falcon; and all these, except the horses, walk about the house, which every now and then resounds with their unarbitrated quarrels, as if they were the masters of it… . [P.S.] I find that my enumeration of the animals in this Circean Palace was defective …. I have just met on the grand staircase five peacocks, two guinea hens, and an Egyptian crane. I wonder who all these animals were before they were changed into these shapes."

From 1821 to 1822, he finished Cantos 6–12 of Don Juan at Pisa, and in the same year he joined with Leigh Hunt and Percy Bysshe Shelley in starting a short-lived newspaper, The Liberal, in the first number of which appeared The Vision of Judgment.

For the first time since his arrival in Italy, Byron found himself tempted to give dinner parties; his guests included the Shelleys, Edward Ellerker Williams, Thomas Medwin, John Taaffe and Edward John Trelawney; and "never", as Shelley said, "did he display himself to more advantage than on these occasions; being at once polite and cordial, full of social hilarity and the most perfect good humour; never diverging into ungraceful merriment, and yet keeping up the spirit of liveliness throughout the evening."

Byron's mother-in-law Judith Noel, the Hon. Lady Milbanke, died in 1822. Her will required that he change his surname to "Noel" in order for him to inherit half of her estate. He obtained a Royal Warrant allowing him to "take and use the surname of Noel only". The Royal Warrant also allowed him to "subscribe the said surname of Noel before all titles of honour", and from that point he signed himself "Noel Byron" (the usual signature of a peer being merely the peerage, in this case simply "Byron").

The Shelley's and Williams had rented a house on the coast and had a schooner built. Byron decided that he too should have his own yacht, and engaged Trelawny's friend, Captain Daniel Roberts, to design and construct the boat. It was named the Bolivar.

On July 8th, 1822 Shelley drowned in a boating accident. Byron attended the funeral. Shelley was cremated on the beach at Viareggio where his body had washed up. His ashes were later interred in Rome in the cemetery in Rome where lay already his son William and John Keats.

Byron was living in Genoa when, in 1823, while growing bored, he accepted a call for his help from representatives of the movement for Greek independence from the Ottoman Empire. With the assistance of his banker and Captain Daniel Roberts, Byron chartered the Brig Hercules to take him to Greece. On 16 July, Byron left Genoa arriving at Kefalonia in the Ionian Islands on August 4th.

Byron had spent £4,000 of his own money to refit the Greek fleet and sailed for Missolonghi in western Greece, arriving on December 29th, to join Alexandros Mavrokordatos, a Greek politician with military power. When the famous Danish sculptor Bertel Thorvaldsen heard about Byron's heroics in Greece, he voluntarily re-sculpted his earlier bust of Byron in Greek marble.

Mavrokordatos and Byron planned to attack the Turkish-held fortress of Lepanto, at the mouth of the Gulf of Corinth. Byron employed a fire-master to prepare artillery and took part of the rebel army under his own command, despite his lack of military experience. Before the expedition could sail, on February 15th, 1824, he fell ill, and the usual remedy of bloodletting weakened him further. He made a partial recovery, but in early April he caught a violent cold which further therapeutic bleeding, insisted on by his doctors, aggravated. He developed a violent fever, and died in Missolonghi on April 19th.

Alfred, Lord Tennyson would later recall the shocked reaction in Britain when word was received of Byron's death. The Greeks mourned Lord Byron deeply, and he became a hero. The Greek form of "Byron", continues in popularity as a name in Greece, and a town near Athens is called Vyronas in his honour.

Byron's body was embalmed, but the Greeks wanted their hero to stay with them. Some say his heart was removed to remain in Missolonghi. His body was returned to England (despite his dying wishes that it should not) for burial in Westminster Abbey, but the Abbey refused to accept it on the grounds of "questionable morality".

Huge crowds viewed his body as he lay in state for two days in London before being buried at the Church of St. Mary Magdalene in Hucknall, Nottinghamshire. A marble slab given by the King of Greece is laid directly above Byron's grave.

Byron's friends had raised the sum of £1,000 to commission a statue of the writer by the sculptor Thorvaldsen. However for a decade after the statue was completed, in 1834, most British institutions had refused to accept it, among them the British Museum, St. Paul's Cathedral, Westminster Abbey and the National Gallery, and it remained in storage. Finally Trinity College, Cambridge, placed the statue in its library.

Finally, in 1969, a145 years after Byron's death, a memorial to him was placed in Westminster Abbey. It had been pointedly noted by the New York Times that "People are beginning to ask whether this ignoring of Byron is not a thing of which England should be ashamed ... a bust or a tablet might be put in the Poets' Corner and England be relieved of ingratitude toward one of her really great sons." At last Byron was where he should be.

Lord Byron – A Concise Bibliography

The Major Works
Hours of Idleness (1807)

English Bards and Scotch Reviewers (1809)
Childe Harold's Pilgrimage, Cantos I & II (1812)
The Giaour (1813)
The Bride of Abydos (1813)
The Corsair (1814)
Lara, A Tale (1814)
Hebrew Melodies (1815)
The Siege of Corinth (1816)
Parisina (1816)
The Prisoner of Chillon (1816)
The Dream (1816)
Prometheus (1816)
Darkness (1816)
Manfred (1817)
The Lament of Tasso (1817)
Beppo (1818)
Childe Harold's Pilgrimage (1818)
Don Juan (1819–1824; incomplete on Byron's death in 1824)
Mazeppa (1819)
The Prophecy of Dante (1819)
Marino Faliero (1820)
Sardanapalus (1821)
The Two Foscari (1821)
Cain (1821)
The Vision of Judgment (1821)
Heaven and Earth (1821)
Werner (1822)
The Age of Bronze (1823)
The Island (1823)
The Deformed Transformed (1824)

Index of Titles (This is an abbreviated, not a complete, list of his poems).
A
Address, spoken at the Opening of Drury-Lane Theatre, Saturday, October 10, 1812
The Adieu
Adieu to the Muse (same as "Farewell to the Muse")
Address intended to be recited at the Caledonian Meeting
Adrian's Address to his Soul when Dying
The Age of Bronze (a transcription project)
"All is Vanity, Saith the Preacher"
And Thou Art Dead, as Young and Fair
And Wilt Thou Weep When I am Low?
Another Simple Ballat
Answer to —'s Professions of Affection
Answer to a Beautiful Poem
Answer to Some Elegant Verses Sent by a Friend to the Author, & etc.
Answer to the Foregoing, Addressed to Miss —
Aristomenes
Away, Away, Ye Notes of Woe!

B

Ballad
Beppo, a Venetian Story
The Blues, a Literary Eclogue
Bowles and Campbell
The Bride of Abydos, a Turkish Tale (A transcription project)
Bright Be the Place of Thy Soul! (see "Stanzas for Music")
By the Rivers of Babylon We Sat Down and Wept
"By the Waters of Babylon"

C

Cain, a Mystery (A transcription project)
The Chain I gave (same as "From the Turkish")
The Charity Ball
Childe Harold's Good Night (from Childe Harold's Pilgrimage, Canto I.)
Childe Harold's Pilgrimage
Childish Recollections
Churchill's Grave
The Conquest
The Cornelian
The Corsair: A Tale
The Curse of Minerva

D

Damætas
Darkness
The Death of Calmar and Orla
The Deformed Transformed, a drama (A transcription project)
The Destruction of Sennacherib
The Devil's Drive
Don Juan
A Dream (same as "Darkness")
The Dream
The Duel

E

E Nihilo Nihil; or, An Epigram Bewitched
Egotism. A Letter to J. T. Becher
Elegiac Stanzas on the Death of Sir Peter Parker, Bart.
Elegy
Elegy on Newstead Abbey
Elegy on the Death of Sir Peter Parker (same "Elegiac Stanzas on the Death of Sir Peter Parker, Bart.")
Endorsement to the Deed of Separation, in the April of 1816
English Bards, and Scotch Reviewers, a Satire
Epigram (If for Silver, or for Gold)
Epigram (In Digging up your Bones, Tom Paine)
Epigram (It Seems That the Braziers Propose Soon to Pass)
Epigram (The world is a bundle of hay)
Epigram on an Old Lady Who Had Some Curious Notions Respecting the Soul
Epigrams (Oh, Castlereagh! Thou Art a Patriot Now)

Epilogue
The Episode of Nisus and Euryalus (A Paraphrase from the Æneid, Lib. 9.)
Epistle from Mr. Murray to Dr. Polidori
Epistle to a Friend
Epistle to Augusta
Epistle to Mr. Murray
Epitaph
Epitaph for Joseph Blacket, Late Poet and Shoemaker
Epitaph for William Pitt
Epitaph on a Beloved Friend
Epitaph on a Friend (same as "Epitaph on a Beloved Friend")
Epitaph on John Adams, of Southwell
Epitaph to a Dog
Euthanasia

F
Fame, Wisdom, Love, and Power Were Mine (same as "All is Vanity, saith the Preacher")
Fare Thee Well
Farewell (same as "Farewell! if Ever Fondest Prayer")
Farewell Petition to J. C. H., Esqre.
Farewell to Malta
Farewell to the Muse
Fill the Goblet Again
The First Kiss of Love
A Fragment (Could I Remount the River of My Years)
Fragment (Hills of Annesley, Bleak and Barren)
A Fragment (When, to Their Airy Hall, my Fathers' Voice)
Fragment from the "Monk of Athos"
Fragment of a Translation from the 9th Book of Virgil's Æneid (compare "The Episode of Nisus and Euryalus")
Fragment of an Epistle to Thomas Moore
Fragments of School Exercises: From the "Prometheus Vinctus" of Æschylus
Francesca of Rimini
Francisca
From Anacreon Ode 3. ('Twas Now the Hour When Night Had Driven)
From Job (same as "A Spirit Passed Before Me")
From the French (Ægle, Beauty and Poet, Has Two Little Crimes)
From the French (Must Thou Go, my Glorious Chief)
From the Last Hill That Looks on Thy Once Holy Dome (same as "On the Day of the Destruction of Jerusalem by Titus")
From the Portuguese
From the Turkish (same as "The Chain I Gave")

G
G. G. B. to E. P. (same as "To M. S. G.") (When I Dream That You Love Me, you'll surely Forgive)
The Giaour
The Girl of Cadiz
Granta. A Medley

H
The Harp the Monarch Minstrel Swept

Heaven and Earth, a Mystery (A transcription project)
Hebrew Melodies
Herod's Lament for Mariamne
Hints from Horace (A transcription project)
Hours of Idleness

I

I Speak Not, I Trace Not, I Breathe Not Thy Name (see "Stanzas for Music")
I Saw Thee Weep
I Would I Were a Careless Child
Ich Dien
If Sometimes in the Haunts of Men
If That High World
Imitated from Catullus
Imitation of Tibullus
Impromptu
Impromptu, in Reply to a Friend
In the Valley of Waters (same as "By the Waters of Babylon")
Inscription on the Monument of a Newfoundland Dog
The Island, or Christian and His Comrades
The Irish Avatar
It is the Hour (compare with first stanza of Parisina)

J

Jeptha's Daughter
John Keats
Journal in Cephalonia
Julian [a Fragment]

K

L

La Revanche
Lachin y Gair
L'Amitié est L'Amour sans Ailes
The Lament of Tasso
Lara: A Tale
Last Words on Greece
Lines Addressed by Lord Byron to Mr. Hobhouse on his Election for Westminster
Lines Addressed to a Young Lady
Lines Addressed to the Rev. J. T. Becher
Lines Inscribed Upon a Cup Formed From a Skull
Lines in the Travellers' Book at Orchomenus
Lines on Hearing That Lady Byron Was Ill
Lines on Sir Peter Parker (same as "Elegiac Stanzas on the Death of Sir Peter Parker, Bart.")
Lines to a Lady Weeping (same as "To a Lady Weeping")
Lines to Mr. Hodgson
Lines Written Beneath a Picture
Lines Written Beneath an Elm in the Churchyard of Harrow
Lines Written in an Album, At Malta
Lines Written in "Letters of an Italian Nun and an English Gentleman

Lines Written on a Blank Leaf of The Pleasures of Memory
Lord Byron's Verses on Sam Rogers
Love and Death
Love and Gold
A Love Song. To — (same as "Remind me not, Remind me not")
Love's Last Adieu
Lucietta. A Fragment

M

Maid of Athens, Ere We Part
Manfred, a Dramatic Poem
Marino Faliero, Doge of Venice, an Historical Tragedy (1821) (A transcription project)
Martial, Lib. I. Epig. I.
Mazeppa
Monody on the Death of the Right Hon. R. B. Sheridan
The Morgante Maggiore (A transcription project)
My Boy Hobbie O
My Epitaph
My Soul is Dark

N

Napoleon's Farewell
Napoleon's Snuff-box
The New Vicar of Bray
Newstead Abbey

O

An Occasional Prologue
Ode from the French
Ode on Venice
Ode to a Lady Whose Lover was Killed by a Ball, Which at the Same Time Shivered a Portrait Next His Heart
Ode to Napoleon Buonaparte
An Ode to the Framers of the Frame Bill
Oh! Snatched Away in Beauty's Bloom
Oh! Weep for Those
On a Change of Masters at a Great Public School
On a Cornelian Heart Which Was Broken
On a Distant View of the Village and School of Harrow on the Hill, 1806
On a Royal Visit to the Vaults (Windsor Poetics)
On Being Asked What Was the "Origin of Love"
On Finding a Fan
On Jordan's Banks
On Leaving Newstead Abbey
On Lord Thurlow's Poems
On Moore's Last Operatic Farce, or Farcical Opera
On My Thirty-third Birthday
On My Wedding-Day
On Napoleon's Escape from Elba
On Parting
On Revisiting Harrow

On Sam Rogers (same as "Lord Byron's Verses on Sam Rogers")
On the Birth of John William Rizzo Hoppner
On the Bust of Helen by Canova
On the Day of the Destruction of Jerusalem by Titus
On the Death of — Thyrza (same as "To Thyrza")
On the Death of a Young Lady
On the Death of Mr. Fox
On the Death of the Duke of Dorset
On the Eyes of Miss A— H—
On the Quotation
On the Star of "the Legion of Honour"
On this Day I complete my Thirty-sixth Year
One Struggle More, and I Am Free
Oscar of Alva
Ossian's Address to the Sun in "Carthon"

P

Parenthetical Address
Parisina
Pignus Amoris
The Prayer of Nature
The Prisoner of Chillon
The Prophecy of Dante, a Poem

Q

Quem Deus Vult Perdere Prius Dementat
Queries to Casuists

R

R. C. Dallas
Remember Him, whom Passion's Power
Remember Thee! Remember thee!
Remembrance
Remind Me Not, Remind Me Not
Reply to Some Verses of J. M. B. Pigot, Esq., on the Cruelty of his Mistress

S

Sardanapalus, a Tragedy (A transcription project)
Saul
She Walks in Beauty
The Siege of Corinth
A Sketch From Life
So We'll Go No More A-Roving
Soliloquy of a Bard in the Country
Sonetto di Vittorelli
Song (Breeze of the Night in Gentler Sighs)
Song (Fill the Goblet Again! For I Never Before)
Song (Maid of Athens, Ere We Part) (same as "Maid of Athens, Ere We Part")
Song (Thou Art Not False, But Thou Art fickle) same as "Thou Art Not False, But Thou Art Fickle")
Song (When I Roved a Young Highlander) (same as "When I Roved a Young Highlander")
Song For the Luddites

Song of Saul Before His Last Battle
Song To the Suliotes
Sonnet On Chillon
Sonnet on the Nuptials of the Marquis Antonio Cavalli with the Countess Clelia Rasponi of Ravenna
Sonnet, to Genevra (Thine eyes' Blue Tenderness, Thy Long Fair Hair)
Sonnet, to Generva (Thy Cheek is Pale with Thought, but Not From Woe). aka "Sonnet, to the Same"
Sonnet to Lake Leman
Sonnet to the Prince Regent
The Spell is Broke, the Charm is Flown!
A Spirit Passed Before Me
Stanzas (And Thou Art Dead, as Young and Fair)
Stanzas (And Wilt Thou Weep When I am Low?) (same as "And Wilt Thou Weep When I Am Low?")
Stanzas (Away, Away, Ye Notes of Woe)
Stanzas (Chill and Mirk is the Nightly Blast) (same as "Stanzas Composed During a Thunderstorm")
Stanzas (Could Love For Ever)
Stanzas (I Would I Were a Careless Child) (same as "I Would I Were a Careless Child")
Stanzas (If Sometimes in the Haunts of Men)
Stanzas (One Struggle More, and I Am Free)
Stanzas (Remember Him, Whom Passion's Power)
Stanzas (Thou Art Not False, but Thou Art Fickle)
Stanzas (Through Cloudless Skies, in Silvery Sheen) (same as "Stanzas Written in Passing the Ambracian Gulf")
Stanzas (When a Man Hath No Freedom to Fight For at Home)
Stanzas Composed During a Thunderstorm
Stanzas For Music (Bright Be the Place of Thy Soul!)
Stanzas For Music (I Speak Not, I Trace Not, I Breathe Not Thy Name)
Stanzas For Music (There Be None of Beauty's Daughters)
Stanzas For Music (There's Not a Joy the World Can Give Like That it Takes Away)
Stanzas For Music (They Say That Hope is Happiness)
Stanzas To — (same as "Stanzas to Augusta": Though the Day of My Destiny's Over)
Stanzas To a Hindoo Air
Stanzas To a Lady, on Leaving England
Stanzas To a Lady, with the Poems of Camoëns
Stanzas To Augusta (When all around grew drear and dark)
Stanzas To Augusta (Though the day of my Destiny's over)
Stanzas To Jessy
Stanzas To the Po
Stanzas To the Same (same as "There was a Time, I need not name")
Stanzas Written in Passing the Ambracian Gulf
Stanzas Written on the Road Between Florence and Pisa
Substitute For an Epitaph
Sun of the Sleepless!
Sympathetic Address to a Young Lady (same as "Lines to a Lady Weeping")

T
The Tear
There Be None of Beauty's Daughters (see "Stanzas for Music")
There Was a Time, I Need Not Name
There's Not a Joy the World Can Give Like That it Takes Away (see "Stanzas for Music")
They say that Hope is Happiness (see "Stanzas for Music")
Thou Art Not False, but Thou Art Fickle

Thou Whose Spell Can Raise the Dead (same as "Saul")
Thoughts Suggested by a College Examination
Thy Days are Done
To — (But Once I Dared to Lift My Eyes)
To — (Oh! Well I Know Your Subtle Sex)
To A— (same as "To M—")
To a Beautiful Quaker
To a Knot of Ungenerous Critics
To a Lady (Oh! Had My Fate Been Join'd with Thine)
To a Lady (This Band, Which Bound Thy yellow Hair)
To a Lady (When Man, Expell'd from Eden's Bowers)
To a Lady Weeping (same as "Lines To a Lady Weeping")
To a Lady who Presented to the Author a Lock of Hair Braided with His Own, and Appointed a Night in December to Meet Him in the Garden
To a Vain Lady
To a Youthful Friend
To an Oak at Newstead
To Anne (Oh, Anne, Your Offences to Me Have Been Grievous)
To Anne (Oh Say Not, Sweet Anne, That the Fates Have Decreed)
To Belshazzar
To Caroline (Oh! When Shall the Grave Hide For Ever My Sorrow?)
To Caroline (Think'st thou I saw thy beauteous eyes)
To Caroline (When I Hear you Express an Affection so Warm)
To Caroline (You Say You Love, and Yet Your Eye)
To D—
To Dives. A Fragment
To E—
To Edward Noel Long, Esq.
To Eliza
To Emma
To E. N. L. Esq. (same as "To Edward Noel Long, Esq.")
To Florence
To George Anson Byron (?)
To George, Earl Delawarr
To Harriet
To Ianthe (The "Origin of Love!"—Ah, why) (same as "On Being Asked What Was the 'Origin of Love'")
To Ianthe (from Canto I of Childe Harold's Pilgrimage) (Not in Those Climes Where I Have Late Been Straying)
To Inez (from Canto I of Childe Harold's Pilgrimage) (Nay, Smile Not at My Sullen Brow)
To Julia (same as "To Lesbia!")
To Lesbia!
To Lord Thurlow
To M—
To Maria — (same as "To Emma")
To Mrs. — (same as "Well! Thou Art Happy")
To Mrs. Musters (same as "Stanzas To a Lady, On Leaving England")
To M. S. G. (When I Dream That You Love Me, You'll Surely Forgive)
To M. S. G. (Whene'er I View Those Lips of Thine)
To Marion
To Mary, on Receiving Her Picture

To Miss E. P. (same as "To Eliza")
To Mr. Murray (For Orford and for Waldegrave)
To Mr. Murray (Strahan, Tonson, Lintot of the Times)
To Mr. Murray (To Hook the Reader, You, John Murray)
To my Son
To Penelope
To Romance
To Samuel Rogers, Esq. (same as "Lines Written On a Blank Leaf of The Pleasures of Memory")
To Sir W. D. (same as "To a Youthful Friend")
To the Author of a Sonnet
To the Countess of Blessington
To the Duke of D— (same as "To the Duke of Dorset")
To the Duke of Dorset
To the Earl of — (same as "To the Earl of Clare")
To the Earl of Clare
To the Honble. Mrs. George Lamb
To the Prince Regent on the Repeal of the Bill of Attainder Against Lord E. Fitzgerald, June, 1819. (same as "Sonnet to the Prince Regent")
To the Rev. J. T. Becher (same as "Lines: Addressed to the Rev. J. T. Becher")
To the Same (same as "And Wilt Thou Weep When I Am Low?")
To the Sighing Strephon
To Thomas Moore (My Boat is on the Shore)
To Thomas Moore (Oh you, Who in all Names Can Tickle the Town)
To Thomas Moore (What Are You Doing Now)
To Thyrza (Without a Stone to Mark the Spot)
To Thyrza (One Struggle More, and I Am Free) (same as "One Struggle More, and I am Free")
To Time
To Woman
Translation from Anacreon Ode 1. (I Wish to Tune My Quivering Lyre)
Translation from Anacreon Ode 5. (Mingle with the Genial Bowl)
Translation from Catullus: Ad Lesbiam
Translation from Catullus: Lugete Veneres Cupidinesque
Translation from Horace
Translation from the "Medea" of Euripides [Ll. 627–660]
Translation from Vittorelli
Translation of a Romaic Love Song
Translation of the Epitaph on Virgil and Tibullus, by Domitius Marsus
Translation of the Famous Greek War Song
Translation of the Nurse's Dole in the Medea of Euripides
Translation of the Romaic Song
The Two Foscari, a Tragedy (A transcription project)

U

V

Venice. A Fragment
Verses Found in a Summer-house at Hales-Owen
Versicles
A Version of Ossian's Address to the Sun
A very Mournful Ballad on the Siege and Conquest of Alhama
Vision of Belshazzar

The Vision of Judgment (A transcription project)
A Volume of Nonsense

W

The Waltz, an Apostrophic Hymn
Warriors and Chiefs! (same as "Song of Saul Before His Last Battle")
We Sate Down and Wept by the Waters of Babel (same as "By the Rivers of Babylon We Sat Down and Wept")
Well! Thou art Happy
Were My Bosom as False as Thou Deem'st It To Be
Werner, or The Inheritance, a Tragedy (A transcription project)
When a Man Hath No Freedom to Fight For at Home (see "Stanzas")
When Coldness Wraps This Suffering Clay
When I Roved a Young Highlander
When We Two Parted
The Wild Gazelle
Windsor Poetics
A Woman's Hair
Written after Swimming from Sestos to Abydos
Written at Athens (same as "The Spell is Broke, the Charm is Flown!")
Written at the Request of a Lady in her Memorandum Book (same as "Lines Written in an Album, At Malta")
Written in an Album (same as "Lines Written in an Album, At Malta")
Written in Mrs. Spencer S.'s— (same as "Lines Written in an Album, At Malta")

www.ingramcontent.com/pod-product-compliance
Lightning Source LLC
Chambersburg PA
CBHW061444040426
42450CB00007B/1210